GLBAL VOICES

Reading the Bible in the Majority World

GLBAL
VOICES

Reading the Bible in the Majority World

Edited by Craig Keener and M. Daniel Carroll R.

Foreword by Edwin Yamauchi

HENDRICKSON PUBLISHERS

Global Voices: Reading the Bible in the Majority World
© 2013 by Hendrickson Publishers Marketing, LLC
P.O. Box 3473
Peabody, Massachusetts 01961-3473

ISBN: 978-1-61970-009-3

Printed in the United States of America

First Printing — January 2013

Library of Congress Cataloging-in-Publication Data

Global voices: reading the Bible in the majority world / edited by
  Craig S. Keener and M. Daniel Carroll R.
       p. cm.
  Includes bibliographical references and indexes.
    ISBN 978-1-61970-009-3 (alk. paper)
    1. Bible—Criticism, interpretation, etc. I. Keener, Craig S., 1960-
  II. Carroll R., M. Daniel.
    BS511.3.G58 2013
    220.6—dc23
                        2012016435

Table of Contents

List of Contributors

J. Ayodeji Adewuya

Professor of New Testament at the Pentecostal Theological Seminary (Cleveland, TN). He is the author of multiple books, including *Holiness and Community in 2 Cor 6:14–7:1—A Study of Paul's View of Communal Holiness in the Corinthians Correspondence* (Peter Lang, 2003). Originally from Nigeria, Dr. Adewuya works cross-culturally in the Philippines and in the United States.

M. Daniel Carroll Rodas

Distinguished Professor of Old Testament at Denver Seminary (Littleton, CO) and adjunct professor at El Seminario Teológico Centroamericano in Guatemala City, Guatemala. His latest book is *Christians at the Border: Immigration, the Church, and the Bible* (Baker Academic, 2008). In addition to Old Testament studies, he has contributed to several publications on the topic of immigration. Dr. Carroll Rodas is half-Guatemalan and is involved in Hispanic ministry.

Daniel K. Darko

Associate Professor of Biblical Studies at Gordon College (Wenham, MA). He is the author of *No Longer Living as the Gentiles: Differentiation and Shared Ethical Values in Ephesians* (T&T Clark, 2008). His research explores contemporary analogies between Ephesians and an African Christian framework and praxis. Dr. Darko is originally from Ghana.

David A. deSilva

Trustees Distinguished Professor at Ashland Theological Seminary (Ashland, OH). He has authored twenty books. One of his most recent publications is *Global Readings: A Sri Lankan Commentary on Paul's Letter to the Galatians* (Cascade, 2011). Dr. deSilva's father is Sinhalese.

Nijay Gupta

Visiting Assistant Professor of New Testament at Eastern University (Philadelphia, PA). He is the author of *Worship That Makes Sense to Paul: A New Approach to the Theology and Ethics of Paul's Cultic Metaphors* (De Gruyter, 2010). His primary area of research is Pauline theology and ethics. Dr. Gupta is of Indian descent.

Craig S. Keener

Professor of New Testament at Asbury Theological Seminary (Wilmore, KY). He is author of fifteen books. One of his recent books, *Miracles: The Credibility of the New Testament Accounts* (Baker Academic, 2011), engages miracle accounts from the Majority World positively in understanding biblical accounts of miracles. Dr. Keener has taught at various institutions internationally, most frequently in Africa, and his wife, Dr. Médine Moussounga Keener, is from the Republic of Congo.

Grant LeMarquand

Anglican Assistant Bishop for the Diocese of Egypt with North Africa and the Horn of Africa, and Area Bishop for the Horn of Africa. Formerly Professor of Biblical Studies and Mission at Trinity School for Ministry (Ambridge, PA). He is the author of *An Issue of Relevance: A Comparative Study of the Story of the Bleeding Woman (Mk 5: 25–34; Mt 9:20–22; Lk 8:43–48) in North Atlantic and African Contexts* (Peter Lang, 2004). Dr. LeMarquand is Canadian.

Barbara M. Leung Lai

Professor of Old Testament and Director of the Pastoral and Chinese Ministry Program, Tyndale University College and Seminary (Toronto, ON). Her most recent publication is *Through the "I"-Window: The Inner Life of Characters in the Hebrew Bible* (Sheffield Phoenix, 2011). Dr. Leung Lai is a first-generation Chinese-Canadian, born and raised in Hong Kong.

Osvaldo Padilla

Assistant Professor of New Testament, Beeson Divinity School (Birmingham, AL). He is the author of *The Speeches of Outsiders in Acts: Poetics, Theology and Historiography* (Cambridge University Press, 2008). Dr. Padilla is a native of the Dominican Republic.

Chloe Sun

Associate Professor of Old Testament Studies, Logos Evangelical Seminary (El Monte, CA). Her publications include *The Ethics of Violence in the Story of Aqhat* (Georgias, 2008). She recently co-edited a contextualized reading on Asian-American women in ministry titled *Mirrored Reflections: Reframing Biblical Characters* (Wipf & Stock, 2010). Dr. Sun is Chinese-American.

Edwin M. Yamauchi

Professor Emeritus of History at Miami University (Oxford, OH). He has published widely in the fields of ancient history, the Old and New Testament, early church history, Gnosticism, and biblical archaeology. One of his most recent works is *Africa and the Bible* (Baker Academic, 2006). Dr. Yamauchi, who was born in Hawaii, is Japanese-American.

K. K. Yeo

Harry R. Kendall Professor of New Testament at Garrett Evangelical Theological Seminary (Evanston, IL) and Academic Director of the International Leadership Group that directs the Christian Studies program at Peking University, China. He has authored more than twenty Chinese books and seven English books on cross-cultural biblical interpretation and Christian spirituality, including *Musing with Confucius and Paul: Toward a Chinese Christian Theology* (Lutterworth, 2008) and *The Spirit Hovers: Journeying through Chaos in Prayers* (Cascade, 2012). He was born and raised on Borneo, Malaysia.

Foreword

Edwin M. Yamauchi

Professor Philip Jenkins has underscored the phenomenal growth of Christianity in the Global South (Latin America, Africa, and Asia). He has also observed that the wholehearted faith in the Bible embraced by Christians in these areas is the key to this growth. As someone who was descended from immigrants from Okinawa to Hawaii, the most racially and culturally diverse state in the union, I can keenly appreciate the insight the writers of the essays in this volume have offered as to the relevance of particular Scriptures to a variety of cultural and ethnic groups throughout the world and to immigrant communities in the United States.

M. Daniel Carroll Rodas, who spent time growing up in Guatemala and has taught there, notes the need for multi-ethnic readings of the Bible both from the great demographic changes making the Global South the majority Christian world, and the increasing challenges of immigrant churches in the United States. He offers some insights into a number of Old Testament passages from a Hispanic diaspora perspective. As marginalized aliens, immigrants can read sympathetically the narratives of Abraham and of Ruth.

Barbara M. Leung Lai, self-consciously as a Chinese "scholar-saint" and "pastor-teacher" who has taught in China, Canada, and many other countries, reads the book of Daniel as a survival guide, contrasting the public Daniel (Dan 1–6) with the private Daniel (Dan 7–12). She has effectively appropriated Daniel's message to not only survive but also flourish in the guild of biblical scholars.

J. Ayodeji Adewuya explicates how important the concept of spiritual warfare found in Ephesians 6:10–18 is to African Christians, in particular to the large numbers of Pentecostal believers. He notes how liberal interpreters have demythologized not only Jesus but also Paul. The role of the Holy Spirit, which has been undervalued in some Western Christian traditions, is of prime significance in the lives of Christians who live in an environment of spiritual oppression.

Grant LeMarquand offers examples of African scholars who were forced to analyze Scriptures as merely academic "specimens" when they did their graduate work in the West, contrary to their own convictions. He presents many examples of the popular use, especially of the Psalms, as "talismans." He notes the appropriation of the imprecatory psalms by African Christians, who have witnessed so much oppression from their enemies. Most African Christians do look to the Scriptures as a "Dragoman," or interpreter, to give them spiritual guidance. He suggests that Christians in the West could show more respect for the Bible as a sacred object, as their casual treatment of the Bible, for example, writing notes on its pages, is a stumbling block to Muslims, who would never treat the Qur'an in this way.

David A. deSilva, who has taught in Sri Lanka and whose father is from there, reports on how Sri Lankan Christians, who come from the majority Buddhist background and from the minority Tamil (Hindu) background, have wrestled with the implications of Galatians. He observes that some teachings of Buddha can be used as anticipations of certain aspects of Christ's teachings. The *stoicheia*, which these Christians must confront, include not only astrology but ethnic and caste divisions, as well as patriarchy. Various aspects of Western Christianity, which include denominational rivalry and Western hymns, are not helpful in nurturing a vibrant local Christianity.

Each of the essays is accompanied by an informative response. Helpful bibliographies are provided to direct readers both to general books on multicultural readings as well as to specific areas discussed. I heartily commend this collection to all biblical scholars as an introduction to the emerging global discussion of the interpretation and application of Scriptures to Christians, wherever they may reside and whatever their backgrounds may be.

Abbreviations

Scripture

CEB	Common English Bible
HB	Hebrew Bible
LXX	Septuagint
NT	New Testament
OT	Old Testament

Journals and Series

AASOR	Annual of the American Schools of Oriental Research
AB	Anchor Bible
AJBS	*African Journal of Biblical Studies*
AJET	*Africa Journal of Evangelical Theology*
AJS	*American Journal of Sociology*
AUS	American University Studies
BBR	*Bulletin for Biblical Research*
BCOTWP	Baker Commentary on the Old Testament Wisdom and Psalms
BDAG	Danker, F. W., W. Bauer, W. F. Arndt, and F. W. Gingrich. *Greek-English Lexicon of the New Testament and Other Early Christian Literature*. 3d ed. Chicago: University of Chicago Press, 2000.
BEC	Baker Exegetical Commentary
BETL	Bibliotheca Ephemeridum Theologicarum Lovaniensium
BibInt	*Biblical Interpretation*
BSac	*Bibliotheca sacra*

BSS	Biblical Studies Series
BTA	Bible and Theology in Africa
CBQ	*Catholic Biblical Quarterly*
CBR	*Currents in Biblical Research*
EH	Europäische Hochschulschriften
EUS	European University Studies
FAT	Forschungen zum Alten Testament
GBS/OT	Guides to Biblical Scholarship
HBM	Hebrew Bible Monographs
IBMR	*International Bulletin of Missionary Research*
IRM	*International Review of Mission*
JBL	*Journal of Biblical Literature*
JOCP	*Journal of Chinese Philosophy*
JETS	*Journal of the Evangelical Theological Society*
JH/LT	*Journal of Hispanic/Latino Theology*
JRAI	*Journal of Religion in Africa*
JPSTC	Jewish Publication Society Torah Commentary
JSNT	*Journal for the Study of the New Testament*
JSOT	*Journal for the Study of the Old Testament*
JTS	*Journal of Theological Studies*
LHB/OTS	Library of Hebrew Bible/Old Testament Studies
MJBS	*Malawi Journal of Biblical Studies*
NICOT	New International Commentary on the Old Testament
NIVAC	New International Version Application Commentary
NTS	*New Testament Studies*
NSBT	New Studies in Biblical Theology
NTSCC	New Testament Studies in Contextual Context
NovT	*Novum Testamentum*
OBT	Overtures to Biblical Theology
OTE	*Old Testament Essays*
OTL	Old Testament Library
PastPsych	*Pastoral Psychology*
PBM	Paternoster Biblical Monographs
PBTM	Paternoster Biblical and Theological Monographs
RSM	Regnum Studies in Mission
SBLSS	Society of Biblical Literature Symposium Series
SBEC	Studies in Bible and Early Christianity

SNTSMS	Society for New Testament Studies Monograph Series
SRA	Studies of Religion in Africa
STI	Studies in Theological Interpretation
VT	*Vetus Testamentum*
WBC	Word Biblical Commentary
ZNW	*Zeitschrift für die neutestamentliche Wissenschaft*

Introduction

Craig S. Keener and M. Daniel Carroll R.

The phenomenal growth of Christianity around the world is now common knowledge.[1] Many estimate that in 1900, just over a century ago, 16.7 percent of Christians lived in Africa, Asia, and Latin America. By 2010 it was 63.2 percent, and by 2025 it will be nearly 70 percent. For some Christian groups, this increase has proved particularly dramatic. For example, evangelicals in these regions have grown from fewer than 50 million in 1960 to nearly 600 million today—already outnumbering evangelicals in the West by four or five times their number.[2]

Yet at the present, Western Christians retain more resources and in academic circles often continue to focus on their own smaller constituencies to the neglect of the needs of the global church. Many experts today argue that it is past time for more Western biblical interpreters to begin passing the baton, to begin partnering with emerging scholars in the Majority World for the sake of the global church.

Confessions of a Western Reader (Craig S. Keener)

When Christians from various cultures enter into dialogue with each other, we often find elements of the biblical message that

---

[1] See, e.g., Philip Jenkins, *The Next Christendom: The Coming of Global Christianity* (New York: Oxford University Press, 2002); idem, *The New Faces of Christianity: Believing the Bible in the Global South* (New York: Oxford University Press, 2006); Jehu J. Hanciles, *Beyond Christendom: Globalization, African Migration, and the Transformation of the West* (Maryknoll, NY: Orbis, 2008).

[2] See Jason Mandryk, *Operation World* (7th ed.; Colorado Springs: Biblica, 2010), 3, 5. Note also statistics in Todd M. Johnson and Kenneth R. Ross, eds., *Atlas of Global Christianity, 1910–2010* (Edinburgh: Center for the Study of Global Christianity, 2009); David B. Barrett, *World Christian Encyclopedia* (2d ed.; New York: Oxford University Press, 2001) and his periodic updating of statistics in *IBMR*.

Christians from any one culture, with their own biases and blinders, have sometimes missed. This has been my experience as a Western Christian. I first dramatically experienced this process when I was doing devotions in Genesis together with my then-fiancée, now my wife, Médine Moussounga Keener. She is from Congo-Brazzaville in Central Africa and has a PhD from the University of Paris. I could supply relevant ancient Near Eastern background for Genesis, but her insights from rural and pastoral culture addressed questions I had not even thought to ask. Médine, who had experience with midwifed childbirths, also was able to resolve my struggle to comprehend several unusual childbirths in Genesis.

More recently, as I was researching a book on miracles, the insights and experiences of Majority World Christians transformed my understanding of some texts that I think I and some other Western scholars sometimes have treated as embarrassments or even tended to allegorize. Rereading these texts from, say, a Nigerian or Chinese lens instead of from a Humean antisupernaturalist one, helped me hear the passages in ways I believe are closer to how first-century Mediterranean hearers would have heard them.[3]

Reflections of a Hybrid Reader (M. Daniel Carroll R.)

I am half-Guatemalan. Part of my journey as a Christian, and then as an OT scholar, has been the effort to sort out what it means to read the Bible in a way that is both honoring to the text and reflective of and relevant to my cultural background. Seminary courses and books on hermeneutics are not always helpful in acknowledging the influence of one's socioeconomic, ethnic, and racial context on interpretation. Interacting with Latin American authors from theological traditions different from my own and with philosophical hermeneutics helped guide me toward a way forward.

The journey continues. What is new—and so encouraging—is that some Western biblical scholars, as never before, are actively engaging points of view from different parts of the globe. They are not judging these readings as simply other interesting perspectives to be added to the growing list of postmodern options that cannot make

---

[3] Craig S. Keener, *Miracles: The Credibility of the New Testament Accounts* (Grand Rapids: Baker Academic, 2011); see esp. 211–358, 513–99.

substantive claims to divine truth. To the contrary, these scholars appreciate these contributions as containing uniquely useful windows into the biblical text, which heretofore have been missed or ignored. This exchange of ideas is becoming a shared enterprise, a mutual learning exercise.

The Background of This Book

Each year the Institute for Biblical Research offers a theme-based program before the Society for Biblical Literature conference. Craig Keener was the program chair for the 2011 annual meeting in San Francisco. His commitments, shared by some others, led to the choice of the theme "Global Readings." The objective of the program was to increase Western biblical interpreters' awareness of perspectives from other parts of the world. A set of voices representing Africa, Asia, and Latin America, coming from several Christian traditions, offered interpretations of passages from both Testaments.

The chapters in this volume follow the sequence of the presentations in San Francisco, beginning with the plenary address given by M. Daniel Carroll R. Each paper had a response—sometimes from a similar culture, sometimes from a different one. To allow greater opportunity for wide-ranging approaches, respondents were asked to not limit their comments to the ideas in the papers to which they had been assigned, but to interact with global biblical interpretation from their own perspectives. Each essay closes with a short list of recommended sources for those who desire to probe this fascinating topic more deeply.

These are only illustrative voices. There are multiple Chinese or Latin American readings, no less than there are numerous Western ones. Cultures also overlap—for example, a Nigerian presenter, who served as a missionary in the Philippines, now teaches in the United States. There also is the growing phenomenon of scholars from hybrid backgrounds, who come from mixed racial and cultural traditions. Some grew up in the West and move across these boundaries in creative ways. In sum, this volume contains a rich selection of interpretations from first-rate biblical scholars from a variety of backgrounds from around the world. We offer these essays as a taste of the fruitful work and constructive conversations that can be generated when the Bible is read with different lenses but with a common commitment to Scripture's unique role in communicating God's message.

The editors appreciate that Hendrickson Publishers recognized the significance of these papers for the ongoing, nascent significance of global biblical studies and invited us to contribute this project as a book. We also would like to thank Jacki Soister, Danny Carroll's graduate assistant at Denver Seminary, for her meticulous work on the indices.

Chapter 1

Reading the Bible through Other Lenses: New Vistas from a Hispanic Diaspora Perspective

M. Daniel Carroll R.

I appreciate very much the opportunity to address my colleagues in biblical studies at this annual meeting of the Institute for Biblical Studies. The topic I was asked to address is an area dear to my person and my vocation as an OT scholar—that is, multiethnic readings of the OT. As some of you know, I am half-Guatemalan. I was raised bilingual and bicultural and spent time in Guatemala growing up. Before assuming my post at Denver Seminary I taught for thirteen years in Guatemala City, and I return there every summer as an adjunct professor. We have established a Spanish-speaking Hispanic program at Denver, and I attend a Hispanic church. Thus, my gratitude for this invitation.

I divide my presentation into three parts. The first offers a picture of current world realities that indicate that the time to listen to and engage multiethnic readings of the Scripture in the West, and specifically the United States, has come. The second suggests a methodological framework from which these kinds of approaches might be done. The third section presents readings of a series of texts that demonstrate their potential to open up new perspectives on the Old Testament. Because of my background and involvements, these examples reflect a Hispanic, or Latino/a, point of view.

The Need to Consider Multiethnic Readings of the Bible

In the last few years there has been a growing interest in multiethnic and global readings. It is not that there has been no interest in the past. For example, African-American biblical and theological studies have

appeared in journals, graced book catalogues, and occupied sessions at
academic conferences for some time. On the world stage, there was for
many years a fascination by some (and opposition by others) with liberation theologies, especially the movement birthed in Latin America and
championed by the Peruvian Gustavo Gutiérrez, the Uruguayan Juan
Luis Segundo, the Brazilian Leonardo Boff, and others. In the 1990s the
Association of Theological Schools organized a globalization initiative
to expand the horizons of North American seminary faculty and administration and incorporated this theme into its accreditation standards.[1]

Nevertheless, it is clear that the scope and rationale of this broader
awareness recently has changed. A few recent high-profile volumes are
indicative of this increased consideration of academic contributions
from different parts of the planet. In 2004 Abingdon produced *The
Global Bible Commentary*; in 2006 Zondervan made available the *Africa
Bible Commentary*; and in 2009 Fortress published *The Africana Bible*.[2]
This marks a major advance: these perspectives are appearing in complete Bible commentaries in the U.S. market, and evangelical publishing
houses are taking part in this altered profile as well. The same also can be
said of multiethnic frameworks from within this country. The appreciation of multiethnic approaches is extending beyond African-American
contributions to include new populations. What has happened and why?

One key factor that has forced this reorientation is the dramatic
change in the demographics of the Christian church over the last few
decades. The inexorable shift of the center of Christianity from what is

labeled the Global North to the Global South (by which is meant Latin
America, Africa, and Asia, and diaspora communities worldwide)[3] is
well known. I will not rehearse the statistics here. Philip Jenkins brought
this reality to the attention of a broad audience in *The Next Christendom:
The Coming of Global Christianity*. Missiologists had been aware of this

---

[1] Alice Frazer Evans, Robert A. Evans, and David A. Roozen, eds., *The Globalization of Theological Education* (Maryknoll, NY: Orbis, 1993).

[2] Daniel Patte, ed., *The Global Bible Commentary* (Nashville: Abingdon,
2004); Hugh R. Page Jr., ed., *The Africana Bible: Reading Israel's Scriptures from
Africa and the African Diaspora* (Minneapolis: Fortress, 2009); Tokunboh Adeyemo, ed., *Africa Bible Commentary* (Grand Rapids: Zondervan, 2006).

[3] There is debate over the proper terminology for this new geographic
context. Options include the Two-Thirds World, the Majority World, and the
Global South. The same is true for how to label this phenomenon within the
church: the Global Church, the World Church.

transformation, but now all were being informed. *The Next Christendom* is in its third edition.[4] In this book Jenkins chronicles the numerical growth of the Christian faith *outside* the West, as well as the migration of believers from those areas *to* the West. It is the latter that are the focus of this essay. These immigrants, refugees, and asylum seekers leave their homelands looking for safety, jobs, and a fresh start for their families; some come with the express purpose to do mission in the West (part of the demographic shift is the rise of mission agencies in the Global South), or they get involved in ministry once they arrive. Expressions and the ethos of Christianity are being reshaped in other latitudes; that different look is coming to these shores, too, and will affect churches and Christian discourse here.

Another of Jenkins's books, *The New Faces of Christianity: Believing the Bible in the Global South,*[5] is particularly pertinent to our topic. A comment he makes in the opening pages is telling: "The more exposure we North Americans and Europeans have to such readings, the harder it might be for us to approach that scripture in the same way again."[6] He characterizes the biblical perspective from those parts of the world as defending a high view of scriptural authority, championing literal interpretations, espousing a conservative morality, embracing the Bible's supernatural depictions of miracles and visions, and identifying closely with the sociopolitical and economic realities of the OT. His point is not simply that the numbers of Majority World Christians and their new-look church cannot be ignored (a thesis of his previous book, which is reinforced in this more recent publication); it is that their take on the Bible cannot either. Its influence on millions of believers and thousands of churches overseas and in our midst is palpable. As an OT scholar, I would add that these perspectives bring different and valid insights into the biblical text that deserve to be heard. The global conversation about the Christian faith has begun in earnest in

---

[4]Philip Jenkins, *The Next Christendom: The Coming of Global Christianity* (3d ed.; Oxford: Oxford University Press, 2011). The first edition was published in 2002. Jenkins continues to nuance his argument in light of reactions to earlier editions. For a different approach to these realities, see Mark A. Noll, *The New Shape of World Christianity: How American Experience Reflects Global Faith* (Downers Grove, IL: InterVarsity Press, 2009).

[5]Philip Jenkins, *The New Faces of Christianity: Believing the Bible in the Global South* (Oxford: Oxford University Press, 2006). His focus is especially Africa and Asia.

[6]Ibid., 17.

evangelical missiological and theological circles;[7] it is just beginning in biblical studies, especially among evangelicals.[8]

A second (and related) factor is the impact of economic globalization. The numerical growth described in the previous paragraphs has to be correlated with world market forces. It is not uncommon to hear glowing reports of the achievements of the global economy, such as the exploding networks of information, the wonders of communication tools not bound by geography, the value of multinational trade agreements, the reform of outdated business practices and structures, and the opportunities for entrepreneurs anywhere to participate in this latest iteration of capitalism (the world is flat, Thomas Friedman tells us).[9] Others speak of the negative costs of this global economy. They warn of the ubiquitous penetration of destructive elements of Western pop culture that undermine local values and religious beliefs, the unfairness of the markets and flow of capital, the loss of the virtue of compassion coupled with cuts in social spending, the pauperization of the masses outside the technological and educational reach of these advances, and the dire ecological effects in nations that put profit before creation care.[10]

---

[7] E.g., William D. Taylor, ed., *Global Missiology for the Twenty-first Century: The Iguassu Dialogue* (Grand Rapids: Baker Academic, 2000); Craig Ott and Harold A. Netlund, eds., *Globalizing Theology: Belief and Practice in an Era of World Christianity* (Grand Rapids: Baker Academic, 2006); Timothy C. Tennent, *Theology in the Context of World Christianity: How the Global Church Is Influencing the Way We Think about and Discuss Theology* (Grand Rapids: Zondervan, 2007); William A. Dyrness and Veli-Matti Kärkkäinen, eds., *Global Dictionary of Theology: A Resource for the Worldwide Church* (Downers Grove, IL: InterVarsity Press, 2008).

[8] Presently, the publishing houses that are considered more mainline (e.g., Abingdon, Westminster John Knox, Fortress) produce the vast majority of publications of multiethnic persuasions.

[9] Thomas L. Friedman, *The Lexus and the Olive Tree: Understanding Globalization* (rev. ed.; New York: Farrar Straus Giroux, 2000); idem, *The World Is Flat: A Brief History of the Twenty-first Century* (New York: Farrar Straus Giroux, 2000).

[10] E.g., Joseph Stiglitz, *Globalization and Its Discontents* (New York: W. W. Norton, 2002); Jeffrey D. Sachs, *The End of Poverty: Economic Possibilities for Our Time* (New York: Penguin, 2005); idem, *The Price of Civilization: Reawakening American Virtue and Prosperity* (New York: Random House, 2011). From Christian perspectives, note, e.g., Max L. Stackhouse and J. Paris, eds., *God and Globalization*, vol. 1: *Religion and the Powers of the Common Life* (Theology for the Twenty-First Century; Harrisburg, PA: Trinity Press International, 2000); M. Daniel Carroll R., "The Challenge of Economic Globalization for Theology:

I am not the one to evaluate these macroeconomic debates, nor is this essay the venue for such an exercise. There is a by-product of globalization, however, that is undeniable and important for us. Economic globalization has generated the movement of millions within nations and to other countries. For a host of reasons, the transfer of goods and ideas has been accompanied by a flow of labor.[11] The International Organization for Migration estimates that today there are more than 200 million migrants worldwide.[12] This population transfer has led to the creation of economically needy, marginalized diaspora communities across the globe. Their experiences of migration from their homelands and their settling into new lands have spawned research in diverse fields in sociology and anthropology, such as diaspora theory, immigration history and legislation, ethnicity and hybridity, assimilation studies, and transnationalism.

One of these diaspora groups includes the millions of Latin Americans who have migrated the last few decades to this country, whether legally or without documentation. "Diaspora" is a better label than "immigrant," as the term encompasses both first-generation immigrants and their communities and their descendants.[13] Millions of Hispanics of this diaspora claim the Christian faith. Their presence has revitalized the Roman Catholic Church, and many Protestant denominations have begun to plant churches, start Hispanic ministries, and establish educational initiatives to meet the needs and tap the potential of this diaspora

---

From Latin America to a Hermeneutics of Responsibility," in *Globalizing Theology: Belief and Practice in an Era of World Christianity* (ed. Craig Ott and Harold A. Netlund; Grand Rapids: Baker Academic, 2006), 199–212.

[11] E.g., Jagdish Bhagwati, *In Defense of Globalization* (New York: Oxford University Press, 2004), 208–18. For the impact on global mission, see Jehu J. Hanciles, *Beyond Christendom: Globalization, African Migration, and the Transformation of the West* (Maryknoll, NY: Orbis, 2008).

[12] Go to http://en.wikipedia.org/wiki/Immigration. Also note Khalid Koser, *International Migration: A Very Short Introduction* (New York: Oxford University Press, 2007).

[13] In this essay I do not engage technical studies on diaspora or migration. For an excellent introduction to the former, see Stéphane Dufoix, *Diasporas* (trans. W. Rodarmor; Berkeley, CA: University of California Press, 2008); for the latter, see Stephen Castles and Mark J. Miller, *The Age of Migration: International People Movements in the Modern World* (4th ed.; New York: Guilford, 2009). Also note the discussion and bibliography in Luis Rivera Rodríguez, "Toward a Diaspora Hermeneutics (Hispanic North America)," in *Character Ethics and the Old Testament: Moral Dimensions of Scripture* (ed. M. Daniel Carroll R. and J. Lapsley; Louisville: Westminster John Knox, 2007), 169–89.

population. The ethnic makeup of this country—and of the Christian faith—is changing rapidly. The face of the United States will be very different in twenty to thirty years.[14]

One challenge from the biblical studies side of things is to try to read the Bible with an eye to its appropriation by these communities. Another is to ask if this diaspora community has its own contribution to make to biblical studies.[15] To maintain business as usual in our research and in our biblical studies departments (recruitment, course offerings, library acquisition budgets, and faculty hirings) is to march into irrelevance. It is not that everything becomes ethnic studies, but it is that multiethnic perspectives do become a factor in ministerial training, preparation of students for cultural engagement, and topics for study. Neither is it to say all minorities can and must do only multiethnic work; I certainly do not want to be put into that box as an OT scholar. It is to say, however, that the context for biblical studies soon will not be the same.

To summarize this first section, multiethnic approaches are needful for at least two reasons. First, worldwide demographic changes demand that other ethnic perspectives, both abroad and at home, be given an attentive hearing. The theology and biblical work of this growing global presence cannot be ignored. The numbers will not allow it. Second, the presence of diaspora communities in this country is part of larger world realities that are having and will continue to have a major effect on national and church life. How might biblical scholarship move forward to engage these new realities?

Methodological Suggestions for a Hispanic Diaspora Reading

The introductory nature of this presentation allows me only to highlight a few items within a larger and more complex hermeneutical and methodological discussion.

To begin with, as I commend a Hispanic diaspora approach for certain readings of the OT, it is important for me to say what I am *not*

---

[14]A helpful and respected source for data is the Pew Hispanic Center (http://pewhispanic.org/).

[15]One might say that this is an instance of the "glocal"—that is, the dynamic and mutual interaction between local expressions of something (here the field of biblical studies) and the wider ("global") field of OT scholarship. "Glocal" is a prominent term in recent missiology.

endorsing. I am well aware that a diaspora approach can be a subset of postcolonial studies. Some of these may have philosophical underpinnings that may be problematic; some turn their critical gaze at the Bible itself, censuring what is felt to be the inherent ideological shortcomings of its production and questioning its unique hegemonic status for Christians.[16] I am not advocating these sorts of approaches, although they do raise challenging questions.

What I find helpful and necessary is the insistence of self-consciously reading the text from a particular place. The rejection of the notion of an objective observer, one detached from and unaffected by social standing, economic status, ethnicity, culture, and gender, is now common, even among evangelicals.[17] A diaspora approach is a specific application of this hermeneutical fact. This perspectival commitment is evident in global evangelical circles, for instance, in a series of consultations on diaspora missions by the Lausanne Movement[18] and the inclusion of diaspora concerns in the Cape Town Commitment document (Section IIC.5) in October 2010.[19] Significant work is being done on the Korean

---

[16] See R. S. Sugirtharajah, *The Bible and the Third World: Precolonial, Colonial, and Postcolonial Encounters* (Cambridge: Cambridge University Press, 2001); idem, "Postcolonial Biblical Interpretation," in *Voices from the Margin: Interpreting the Bible in the Third World* (ed. R. S. Sugirtharajah; 3d ed.; Maryknoll, NY: Orbis, 2006), 64–84. There also are internal debates within these circles. Some feel that postcolonial scholars, Sugirtharajah in particular, have wrongly severed connections to liberation theology. See Gerald O. West, "What Difference Does Postcolonial Biblical Criticism Make? Reflections from a (South) African Perspective," in *Postcolonial Interventions: Essays on Honor of R. S. Sugirtharajah* (ed. B. Liew; The Bible in the Modern World 23; Sheffield: Sheffield Phoenix Press, 2009), 256–73. Fernando F. Segovia tracks these changes in "Tracing Sugirtharajah's Voice from the Margin: From Liberation to Postcolonialism," in *Postcolonial Interventions* 215–39. For applications to OT research, see Bradley L. Crowell, "Postcolonial Studies and the Hebrew Bible," *CBR* 7, no. 2 (2009): 217–43.

[17] Kevin J. Vanhoozer discusses these issues within the new global context in "'One Rule to Rule Them All?' Theological Method in an Era of World Christianity," in *Globalizing Theology: Belief and Practice in an Era of World Christianity* (ed. Craig Ott and Harold A. Netlund; Grand Rapids: Baker Academic, 2006), 85–126.

[18] Go to http://www.lausanne.org/en/gatherings/issue-based/diasporas-2009.html.

[19] See the document at http://www.lausanne.org/en/documents/ctcommitment.html.

and African diaspora here and in different parts of the world,[20] and there will be more in the future. I will focus on the Hispanic community.

Several features characterize diaspora Hispanic interpretation of the Bible.[21] A helpful introduction to these matters is offered by Cuban-American scholar Justo González. In *Santa Biblia* he lists five characteristics of reading the Bible with "Hispanic eyes."[22] Although he acknowledges that one should not generalize too easily about how Hispanics read, González suggests that those who interact with the text with their identity and heritage in mind do so from these perspectives, or paradigms:

Marginality. This refers to identifying with characters who are on the margins of biblical narratives, or reading passages from personal experiences of social marginalization and exclusion.

Poverty. Many who come to this country do so to escape poverty, but they continue to be poor after their arrival. The imperative in the reading of Scripture is to be aware of poverty issues in the text and sensitive to those of the community.

Mestizaje.[23] The term *mestizaje* refers to the descendants of the mixed ethnicity of the Spanish with the indigenous and that

---

[20] For the Korean diaspora, see Wonsuk Ma and S. Hun Kim, eds., *Korean Diaspora and Christian Mission* (RSM; Oxford: Regnum; Eugene, OR: Wipf & Stock, 2011); for the African, see Hanciles, *Beyond Christendom.* Note a recent issue of *Transformation* (28, no. 1 [2011]), which looks at diaspora issues in Europe.

[21] Many Hispanic churches do not *consciously* shape their theology or ecclesiology according to these features, as they are grounded formally in very different paradigms (e.g., traditional systematic theology, health and wealth gospel, manifestations of neo-Pentecostalism).

[22] Justo L. González, *Santa Biblia: The Bible through Hispanic Eyes* (Nashville: Abingdon, 1996). Also see Pablo A. Jiménez, "The Bible: An Hispanic Perspective," in *Teología en Conjunto: A Collaborative Hispanic Protestant Theology* (ed. José David Rodríguez and Loida I. Martell-Otero; Louisville: Westminster John Knox, 1997), 66–79; Luis G. Pedraja, *Teología: An Introduction to Hispanic Theology* (Nashville: Abingdon, 2003); Carmen Nanko-Fernández, *Theologizing in Espanglish: Context, Community, and Ministry* (Maryknoll, NY: Orbis, 2010).

[23] González also mentions *mulatez*, the mixture of Anglo and African or African with indigenous.

of Latin Americans with North Americans. This lens alerts the reader to ethnic complexities within the biblical accounts, which also might speak to the contemporary context.

As exiles and aliens. The Bible describes lives of the people of God far from home. These portrayals find an echo among Hispanics and can point to lessons for faith and survival.

Solidarity. Hispanic valorization of family and community engenders a special appreciation for the communal exhortations and shared life in both Testaments. These affect the perception of the role of the local church as extended family.

Luis Rivera Rodríguez, a Puerto Rican scholar, has a more elaborate presentation of diaspora hermeneutics.[24] For one, he grounds his work in a thorough interaction with social science research on diasporic communities. From this framework Rivera Rodríguez describes in some detail the multidirectional dynamics operative in these communities (translocality, communality, transnationality, interculturality, marginality, and diaspolitics) and applies them to biblical studies. In a complex, though comprehensive, summary he depicts diaspora hermeneutics as[25]

> one in which the diasporic situation and location, the diasporic human condition, and a diasporic sociopolitical project (represented historically or symbolically in texts and experienced by the readers) become key interpretive concerns and entries for the exploration and interpretation of the meaning and function of the text done by diasporic people in their quest to produce meaning, reproduce their social locations and identities, and determine ways to act politically and religiously as members of diasporic communities and congregations.

---

[24] Rivera Rodríguez, "Toward a Diaspora Hermeneutics (Hispanic North America)"; cf. idem, "Immigration and the Bible: Comments by a Diasporic Theologian," *Perspectivas* 10 (2006): 23–36. Rivera Rodríguez acknowledges his debt to Fernando F. Segovia. See, e.g., Fernando F. Segovia, "Toward a Hermeneutics of Diaspora: A Hermeneutics of Otherness and Engagement," in *Reading from This Place,* vol. 1: *Social Location and Biblical Interpretation in the United States* (ed. Fernando F. Segovia and Mary Ann Tolbert; Minneapolis: Fortress, 1995), 57–73.

[25] Rivera Rodríguez, "Toward a Diaspora Hermeneutics (Hispanic North America)," 179.

The interpreter, then, looks for diaspora material in the Bible in order to discover insights about God and about diasporic individual, family, communal, and religious life. There the interpreter finds experiences that parallel in some degree those of Hispanics—their marginalization, their fears, challenges, and tensions vis-à-vis the majority culture, and their longings for their homeland—as well as lessons about how not to treat the "other." The biblical and contemporary contexts and experiences of diaspora are analogous, not identical. This orientation can lead to fresh understandings and appropriations of the text.

Permit me two brief observations about the role and vocation of Hispanic scholars who are committed to reading *latinamente* from and for our communities, even as we are involved with them in *lo cotidiano* (the stuff of everyday life). First, in spite of the diverse national heritages that make up Latin America and from which Hispanic scholars trace their roots, there is a strong value placed on doing scholarship *en conjunto*—that is, together in collaboration with other Hispanic scholars across discipline, denominational, and ecclesial boundaries in the effort to work for the common good.[26] Second, OT scholar Jean-Pierre Ruiz rightly has sounded the call to do responsible academic work that is both self-critical and accountable to the wider scholarly guild and that is in constructive conversation even with those who might hold contrary positions to matters related to the Hispanic community.[27]

One final comment. As I move to the third part of this presentation, I ask for a hermeneutical charity that exhibits the virtues of respect and patience in engaging Hispanic interpretations of the text and the vistas of the Bible it might open up.[28] Respect, not only in the sense of a willingness to listen, but also respect and patience for what might be a different emphasis from which one may learn and grow. Such respect will lead neither to marginalization by exclusion nor to domestication by inclusion (making this just another interpretive option among many that need not be taken overly seriously). Both responses effectively

---

[26] Note the title of the volume edited by José Rodríguez and Martell-Otero: *Teología en Conjunto: A Collaborative Hispanic Protestant Theology.*

[27] Jean-Pierre Ruiz, *Reading from the Edges: The Bible and People on the Move* (Maryknoll, NY: Orbis, 2011), 13–53.

[28] I am appropriating the argument of Richard S. Briggs in *The Virtuous Reader: Old Testament Narrative and Interpretive Virtue* (STI; Grand Rapids: Baker Academic, 2010) to interpretations of the biblical text and the constructive lens that Hispanic readings might bring to the reading of the OT.

silence these perspectives. Multiethnic voices bring their views to the academic table with the hope of enjoying scholarly hospitality and engagement by peers.[29] The experience of not being heard or taken into account has frustrated scholars from other parts of the world for decades;[30] my hope is that this disappointment is not repeated with Hispanic biblical studies.[31]

Readings of Old Testament Narratives from a Hispanic Diaspora Perspective

The readings that follow are based on the final form of the biblical text. I will not speculate about the possible contexts of the production of these texts and the significance of that for what I will highlight. That, of course, would add another layer of discussion to what is presented here. I also will present readings of these texts in their canonical order. I occasionally refer to background studies and relevant social science research, but most of that appears in footnotes.[32]

---

[29] Biblical presentations designed to inform the immigration debate are another arena, here and in other parts of the world. The focus here is different. See my work cited below in fn. 32. Also note, e.g., in the UK: Nick Spencer, *Asylum and Immigration: A Christian Perspective on a Polarized Debate* (Milton Keynes: Paternoster, 2004); Spain: José Antonio Martínez Díez, *El cristiano ante la migración* (Madrid: Editorial PPC, 2008); Latin America: José E. Ramírez-Kidd, *El extranjero, la viuda y el huérfano en el Antiguo Testamento* (Guatemala City, Guatemala: CEDEPCA; San José, Costa Rica: Universidad Bíblica Latinoamericana, 2003).

[30] Note the comments, e.g., by African scholars Kwame Bediako, *Christianity in Africa: The Renewal of a Non-Western Religion* (Studies in World Christianity; Maryknoll, NY: Orbis, 1996); Tite Tiénou, "Christian Theology in and Era of World Christianity," in *Globalizing Theology: Belief and Practice in an Era of World Christianity* (ed. Craig Ott and Harold A. Netlund; Grand Rapids: Baker Academic, 2006), 37–51.

[31] See the acute observations by Catholic theologian Carmen Nanko-Fernández in relationship to her ecclesial tradition in *Theologizing in Espanglish*. Similar experiences are not uncommon in other traditions as well.

[32] For more extensive presentations, see M. Daniel Carroll R., *Christians at the Border: Immigration, the Church, and the Bible* (Grand Rapids: Baker Academic, 2008, translated as *Cristianos en la frontera: La inmigración, la Iglesia y la Biblia* [Lake Mary, FL: Casa Creación, 2009]); "How to Shape Christian Perspectives on Immigration? Strategies for Communicating Biblical Teaching," in *Religion, Migration, and the Borderlands* (ed. S. Azaransky; Lanham, MD: Lexington, forthcoming); "Looking at the Challenges of Immigration through

What is it like to read the OT from a Hispanic diaspora perspective? The question is significant enough for the American Bible Society to produce a version of the Reina Valera (1960), the most common version in Latin America and the United States, with the cover title *Dios camina con el inmigrante* ("God walks with the immigrant"), which has an eight-page introductory section of Bible passages and comments directed to that population. Let us pursue this line of thought.

Abram, later Abraham, is the father of our faith, and his trust in God (Gen 15:6; cf. 22:15–18) is commended to us (Rom 4; Gal 3). He appears in the biblical account as one on the move, from Ur to the land of Canaan (Gen 11:31–12:9), but once there he would not live a sedentary life. He would buy a plot of ground to bury Sarah, and in his transaction for that property with Ephron the Hittite he declares, "I am an immigrant and a temporary resident (*ger vetôshab*) with you" (CEB). This faith we are to look to was forged by Abraham as a perpetual outsider in that landless existence. The language of this passage is repeated in 1 Pet 2:11 to refer to Christians (cf. 1 Pet 1:1). Scholars differ on what these words might reveal about the socioeconomic and legal standing of those first-century believers,[33] but at the least they stand as a metaphor for the life of all Christians, those "strangers in a strange land," whose citizenship and ultimate loyalties should lie elsewhere (Phil 3:20; Heb 13:14). For immigrants and those in the diaspora this metaphor is not just an abstract, theological description; they live that metaphor every day. They experience the vulnerability and dependency in the spiritual, social, economic, cultural, and familial realms. Can these realities open up constructive insights from the Bible for all who read it?

Soundings in Genesis

I begin this survey of readings with two scenes from Genesis. The first is Abram's move to Egypt because of a famine in the land (Gen

---

a Missional Lens," in *Missional Ethics: Biblical and Theological Perspectives* (ed. J. Rowe and A. Draycott; Downers Grove, IL: InterVarsity Press, forthcoming).

[33] See the different views, e.g., of John H. Elliott, *A Home for the Homeless: A Sociological Exegesis of 1 Peter, Its Situation and Strategy* (Minneapolis: Fortress, 1990); idem, *1 Peter* (AB 37B; New York: Doubleday, 2000); Karen H. Jobes, *1 Peter* (BEC; Grand Rapids: Baker Academic, 2005); Benjamin H. Dunning, *Aliens and Sojourners: Self as Other in Early Christianity* (Philadelphia: University of Pennsylvania Press, 2009).

12:10–20); the second is Joseph's interaction with his brothers in their first trip to Egypt for food during another time of hunger (42:1–26).[34]

Commentators (and ethicists!) have long wrestled with Abram's trek to Egypt to sojourn there with his wife and clan (Gen 12). Fearful for his life, because he supposes Pharaoh will want to take Sarai, Abram tells her to say to him that he is her brother, not her husband. There is some truth to this statement, as they are related (20:12), but still his response to this quandary appears to compromise his faith and his moral obligation to his wife. At one level, one can understand the outcome in this passage (12:16–20) as a demonstration of Yahweh's sovereign protection of the seed in accordance with the promises of 12:1–3,[35] but the ethical problem at the human level remains.

Several scholars recognize the precarious position in which Abram finds himself. Claus Westermann states, "As one who has to beg for food, Abraham has no rights." Westermann goes on to say that to save his and her lives, the patriarch uses the kind of ruse used by the powerless.[36] Others, harking back to medieval commentators, propose that with this ploy Abram can delay the loss of Sarai and save himself, since customarily one would have to obtain permission from the brother for marriage.[37] Feminist scholars scold Abram for objectifying Sarai and using her as a commodity for personal gain.[38]

---

[34] For Egypt's treatment of outsiders, see Anthony Leahy, "Ethnic Diversity in Ancient Egypt," in *Civilizations of the Ancient Near East* (ed. J. M. Sasson, 4 vols. in 2 books; Peabody, MA: Hendrickson, 1995), 4:52–76; James K. Hoffmeier, *Israel in Egypt: The Evidence for the Authenticity of the Exodus Tradition* (New York: Oxford University Press, 1996), 52–106; idem, *The Immigration Crisis: Immigrants, Aliens, and the Bible* (Wheaton, IL: Crossway, 2009), 38–46; K. A. Kitchen, *The Historical Reliability of the Old Testament* (Grand Rapids: Eerdmans, 2003), 343–52. Although I appreciate Hoffmeir's contributions at this point, I do not agree with the thesis of *The Immigration Crisis* that the biblical material focuses only on legal immigrants.

[35] Allen P. Ross, *Creation and Blessing: A Guide to the Study and Exposition of the Book of Genesis* (Grand Rapids: Baker, 1987), 270–73; Nahum M. Sarna, *Genesis* (JPSTC; Philadelphia: The Jewish Publication Society, 1997), 94.

[36] Claus Westermann, *Genesis 1–26* (trans. J. J. Scullion; Continental Commentary; Minneapolis: Augsburg, 1984), 164.

[37] Umberto Cassuto, *A Commentary on the Book of Genesis* (trans. I. Abrahams; 2 vols.; Jerusalem: Magnes Press, 1964), 2:348–52; cf. Sarna, *Genesis*, 95.

[38] E.g., Fokkelien van Dijk-Hemmes, "Sarai's Exile: A Gender-Motivated Reading of Genesis 12.10—13.2," in *A Feminist Companion to Genesis* (ed.

Another perspective to consider from the human side is that desperation yields audacious, even scandalous, actions. It must be remembered that there was a famine. Abram had to feed his clan and care for his animals. They already had traveled a long distance through inhospitable terrain to get to the border with Egypt. If one has to lie to get across in such circumstances (do they just turn around and go back?) and if this puts people in danger, then that is what must be done. Survival is the end game.

There are many such tales of frantic behavior and ethically difficult choices made by those who cross the deserts along our southern border. In his investigative work *Dying to Cross,* Jorge Ramos recounts the horrific experience of the death of nineteen men, women, and children out of seventy who had crammed into the back of a trailer and died from heat and suffocation. One could mention Rubén Martínez's *Crossing Over*, Luis Alberto Urrea's *The Devil's Highway*, Sonia Nazario's award-winning *Enrique's Journey*, and Tim Gaynor's *Midnight on the Line*, and many more testimonies of what people will go through to gain entry and how they engage and try to bypass border authorities.[39] Christian perspectives on these trying treks are multiplying. Recent works include Miguel De La Torre's *Trails of Hope and Terror* and Ben Daniel's *Neighbor*.[40] The point is that hunger drives people to do things that they normally would never do; too much is at stake to have reasoned moral discourse and decide between easy solutions.

Women are most at risk. They sometimes are the more vulnerable members of those who come, some carrying their children; they can be exposed to rape and abuse on the dangerous way to and beyond the border. But they are willing to go through this and participate in deception and

---

A. Brenner; Sheffield: Sheffield Academic Press, 1993), 222–34. The author also mentions the power differences between Abram and Pharaoh.

[39] Jorge Ramos, *Dying to Cross: The Worst Immigrant Tragedy in American History* (trans. K. Cordero; New York: Rayo, 2005); Rubén Martínez, *Crossing Over: A Mexican Family on the Migrant Trail* (New York: Metropolitan, 2001); Luis Alberto Urrea, *The Devil's Highway* (New York: Back Bay, 2004); Sonia Nazario, *Enrique's Journey: The Story of a Boy's Dangerous Odyssey to Reunite with His Mother* (New York: Random House, 2006); Tim Gaynor, *Midnight on the Line: The Secret Life of the U.S.-Mexican Border* (New York: Thomas Dunne, 2009).

[40] Miguel De La Torre, ed., *Trails of Hope and Terror* (Maryknoll, NY: Orbis, 2009); Ben Daniel, *Neighbor: Christian Encounters with "Illegal" Immigration* (Louisville: Westminster John Knox, 2010).

anything else if they believe that it will meet the family's needs.[41] Have we considered this biblical episode of the trickster Abram as the tale of a desperate family at a border crossing? Ruiz's comments are to the point:[42]

> The moral clarity of the regulations in the Hebrew Bible regarding the treatment of aliens becomes considerably muddled as these aliens themselves become implicated in the tension between disclosure and non-disclosure, between the truth and trickery that are essential to survival in the borderlands, the life-and-death tension at the barbed-wire boundary between truth and trickery where the collateral damage is considerable, and where the most vulnerable also become the most expendable.

A diaspora point of view also may offer a different appreciation of the encounter between Joseph and his brothers. In Gen 42 there is famine once again in the land. Hearing that there is food in Egypt, Jacob sends ten of his sons there to buy grain. Since Joseph is the one in charge of the distribution of grain, they are brought before him. They do not recognize him, but he does them. He understands the conversation between them but uses the façade of an interpreter (42:8, 24).

Now Joseph was assimilated into Egyptian culture. He obviously had to speak Egyptian to carry out his tasks; he was given an Egyptian name, married an Egyptian (41:45), and had children by her (41:50). Later he would have Jacob embalmed and would be himself upon his death (50:3, 26). His brothers did not recognize him, probably because Joseph would have worn official garb and may have shaved his head and painted his face in a manner commensurate with his status. Yet, in all of this he gave his sons Israelite names (41:51–52) and maintained his family loyalties, his mother tongue, and a desire to be buried in his homeland. Assimilation did not mean severing his roots. This bilingual, cultural hybrid was God's instrument to preserve his people and help Egypt endure its famine. Do we demand that those who come forsake their language and their past? Many of us are bilingual, bicultural, and can contribute to the common good because of who we are.[43]

---

41 Ruiz, *Reading from the Edges*, 57–70.

42 Ibid., 69–70.

43 Cf. Francisco García-Treto, "Hyphenating Joseph: A View of Genesis 39–41 from the Cuban Diaspora," in *Interpreting beyond Borders* (ed. Fernando F. Segovia; The Bible and Postcolonialism 3; Sheffield: Sheffield Academic Press, 2000), 134–45.

Ruth and the Trials of Assimilation

There are several ways to approach the book of Ruth.[44] One can highlight the legislative background of the gleaning, inheritance, redemption, and levirate laws that inform the actions in the account.[45] Its theological foundations lie in divine and interhuman *hesed*, and commentators correctly stress this dimension of the text.[46] More recent studies attend to the complexity of the characters of the book—their internal wrestlings and their ambiguous interactions with others in Bethlehem and with God.[47]

Some of these dense interpersonal features resonate with what one finds with recently arrived immigrants. Assimilation theory—that is, the study of the processes by which immigrants learn appropriate sociocultural competencies in order to navigate within and integrate into their new context—can be helpful here. Assimilation theory posits that there are three mechanism clusters to accomplish the objective of moving into a different cultural context: purposive action, networks and forms of human capital, and institutional avenues. One can engage the book of Ruth through this grid.[48]

---

[44] For a survey of readings of Ruth from other cultural contexts, coupled with a postcolonial perspective and an argument for an "inclusive hermeneutic," see Cheryl B. Anderson, *Ancient Laws and Contemporary Controversies: The Need for Inclusive Biblical Interpretation* (Oxford: Oxford University Press, 2009), 59–65, 70–77. Other African perspectives are available ad loc. in Patte, *Global Bible Commentary*; Adeyemo, *Africa Bible Commentary*; Page, *Africana Bible*.

[45] For a helpful treatment, see Robert L. Hubbard Jr., *The Book of Ruth* (NICOT; Grand Rapids: Eerdmans, 1988), 48–63.

[46] E.g., Hubbard, *The Book of Ruth*, 66–74, *passim*; Edward F. Campbell Jr., *Ruth* (AB 7; Garden City, NY: Doubleday, 1975), 28–32, *passim*.

[47] Danna Nolan Fewell and David Miller Gunn, *Compromising Redemption: Relating Characters in the Book of Ruth* (Literary Currents in Biblical Interpretation; Louisville: Westminster John Knox, 1990); Tod Linafelt, "Ruth," in Tod Linafelt and Timothy K. Beal, *Ruth, Esther* (Berit Olam; Collegeville, MN: Liturgical Press, 1999); Kristin Moen Saxegaard, *Character Complexity in the Book of Ruth* (FAT 2/47; Tübingen: Mohr Siebeck, 2010).

[48] For more details, see M. Daniel Carroll R., "Once a Stranger, Always a Stranger? Immigration, Assimilation, and the Book of Ruth," a paper presented at the annual meeting of the Society of Biblical Literature in New Orleans, November 2009. The essay cites several studies that investigate the integration processes of Hispanic immigrants into the United States. These continue apace. See Hannah Gill, *The Latino Immigration Experience in North Carolina: New*

Purposive action. In a celebrated speech, Ruth opts to go to Bethlehem with Naomi (1:14–18). Is this solely a statement of loyalty to her mother-in-law and a decision to follow her god? Could it be that Ruth is reticent to return to her own kin? Would there have been a stigma for having married an immigrant from Judah and not having borne him any children? Was she sterile? May hers have been a determination to do whatever was necessary to make a new life for herself in Judah? Why doesn't Naomi respond to Ruth's statement? Along with her bitterness toward God, does Naomi harbor resentment toward what has happened in Moab, such that she desires to get away from Moab and its people? Is she suspicious of Ruth's motives? Ruth also takes the initiative to work in the fields and then quickly responds to Boaz's gestures (Ruth 2); she does not remain silent per Naomi's advice and, at great personal risk, tells Boaz what he must do for the family (Ruth 3).

Network and forms of human capital. In her new land, Ruth has to deal with her mother-in-law and her kinsman, the reapers, the elders, and the women of the town. By the end of chapter 4 she has won the respect of them all, perhaps even of Naomi, although the reader wonders. Naomi is still silent, even when the women declare that Ruth loves her more than seven sons (4:15). She does, though, accept Ruth's son and takes little Obed onto her lap (4:16–17). Surely, this boy, this half-breed, will not have to work as hard as his immigrant mother did to find a place in that world.

Institutional avenues. These entry points are the legal elements at work in the story: the gleaning laws, inheritance, redemption, and levirate marriage. Each of these permits Ruth's access into that agrarian community, and she seems to be aware enough to employ them to advantage.

Still, throughout the assimilation process that one can track as the account progresses, ethnic boundaries are maintained. The townspeople never refer to Ruth by name. To the reapers she is the "young Moabite woman" (Ruth 2:6); to the people and elders at the gate, she is "the woman" (4:11) and "this young woman" (4:12); to the women, "your daughter-in-law" (4:15). In other words, Ruth is *among* them and

---

Roots in the Old North State (Chapel Hill, NC: University of North Carolina Press, 2010); Helen B. Marrow, *New Destination Dreaming: Immigration, Race, and Legal Status in the Rural American South* (Stanford: Stanford University Press, 2011). It might be fruitful to consider the strategies of the powerless used by Ruth. See James C. Scott, *Domination and the Arts of Resistance: Hidden Transcripts* (New Haven: Yale University Press, 1990).

appreciated *by* them, but is she *of* them? Naomi is tender to her at times, calling her "my daughter" (2:2, 22; 3:1, 16, 18), but there are those awkward moments of silence at the beginning and close of the story. This poor woman of interest will become Boaz's wife, but she remains even for him—at least in public—"Ruth the Moabite" (4:5, 10).[49]

Integration is hard and full of challenging relationships and complicated moments. Converse with first-generation immigrants and hear their stories about the strangeness of this landscape and its ways and the embarrassment of their children in this odd zone of being from two places at once . . . and from neither at the same time. Hispanic literature is full of stories of the predicaments of personal and community identity. Authors like Sandra Cisneros of Mexican heritage, Francisco Goldman who struggles with his Guatemalan side, and Julia Álvarez with her Dominican Republic background come to mind.[50]

Lastly, scholars debate the significance of the book's closing genealogy for the purpose and canonical placement of the book (4:18–22). This is important, but to diaspora readers it can communicate that they may be part of a bigger story, part of a grander plan of God, that they cannot even begin to imagine.

Snapshots for Further Reflection

I conclude this section with brief comments on a few other texts that might demonstrate further the value of a diaspora perspective. I concentrate on those that describe exilic and postexilic realities, as these most naturally flow into diaspora approaches.[51]

---

[49] Timothy H. Lim suggests that the author deliberately portrays Ruth as having imperfect Hebrew at Ruth 2:21 in "How Good Was Ruth's Hebrew? Ethnic and Linguistic Otherness in the Book of Ruth," in *The "Other" in Second Temple Judaism: Essays in Honor of John J. Collins* (ed. D. C. Harlow et al.; Grand Rapids: Eerdmans, 2011), 101–15.

[50] Sandra Cisneros, *Caramelo or Puro Cuento* (New York: Vintage, 2002); Francisco Goldman, *The Long Night of White Chickens* (New York: Atlantic Monthly, 1992); Julia Álvarez, *How the García Girls Lost Their Accent* (New York: Plume, 1992) and *Once Upon a Quinceañera: Coming of Age in the U.S.A.* (New York: Viking, 2007).

[51] See Rivera Rodríguez, "Toward a Diaspora Hermeneutics (Hispanic North America)"; cf. Fernando F. Segovia, "In the World but Not of It: Exile as a Locus for a Theology of Diaspora," in *Hispanic/Latino Theology: Challenge and Promise* (ed. Fernando F. Segovia and A. M. Isasi-Díaz; Minneapolis: Fortress,

Nehemiah. The book of Nehemiah is fruitful for discussions on ethnicity. Of course, scholarly interest in ethnicity in the HB span all the way from Israel's beginnings to the postexilic period.[52] Nehemiah can serve an extended case study for at least two fields. First, transnationalism.[53] Although the Jewish diaspora had been removed from their homeland for generations, Nehemiah is still committed to it. He waits for news and then will go to Jerusalem for a time to rebuild its walls and serve as governor. Second, the problem of intermarriage in Neh 13 (cf. Ezra 9–10) provides an opportunity to explore the nature of cultural boundaries, language, religious integrity, and ethnic survival.[54]

1996), 195–217; Gregory Lee Cuellar, *Voices of Marginality: Exile and Return in Second Isaiah 40–55 and the Mexican Immigrant Experience* (AUS 7/271; New York: Peter Lang, 2008). Many find helpful Daniel L. Smith-Christopher, *Religion of the Landless: The Social Context of the Babylonian Exile* (OBT; Minneapolis: Fortress, 1989) and *A Biblical Theology of Exile* (OBT; Minneapolis: Fortress, 2002).

[52] Note the survey in James C. Miller, "Ethnicity and the Hebrew Bible: Problems and Prospects," *CBR* 6, no. 2 (2008): 170–213. Works on ethnicity, whether with a theoretical or anthropological focus, continue to appear. Recent works that postdate Miller's survey include, e.g., William G. Dever, "Ethnicity and the Archaeological Record: The Case of Early Israel," in *The Archaeology of Difference: Gender, Ethnicity, Class, and the "Other" in Antiquity* (ed. D. R. Edwards and C. T. McCollough; AASOR 60/61; Boston: American Schools of Oriental Research, 2007), 49–66; Thomas E. Levy, "Ethnic Identity in Biblical Edom, Israel, and Midian: Some Insights from Mortuary Contexts in the Lowlands of Edom," in *Exploring the Longue Durée: Essays in Honor of Lawrence E. Stager* (ed. J. D. Schloen; Winona Lake, IN: Eisenbrauns, 2009), 251–61; Dermot Anthony Nestor, *Cognitive Perspectives on Israelite Identity* (LHB/OTS 519; New York: T&T Clark, 2010); Louis C. Jonker, ed., *Historiography and Identity (Re)formulation in Second Temple Historiographical Literature* (LHB/OTS 534; New York: T&T Clark, 2010).

[53] For introductions to this field of study, see Peggy Levitt, "Transnational Migration: Taking Stock and Future Directions," *Global Networks* 1, no. 3 (2001): 195–216; Roger Waldinger and David Fitzgerald, "Transnationalism in Question," *AJS* 109, no. 5 (2004): 1177–95; Ewa Morawska, "Transnationalism," in *The New Americans: A Guide to Immigration Since 1965* (ed. M. C. Waters and R. Ueda; Cambridge: Harvard University Press, 2007), 149–63.

[54] For a Hispanic perspective on Neh 13, see Ruiz, *Reading from the Edges,* 100–114. Ethnic approaches to the passage include Smith-Christopher, *A Biblical Theology of Exile,* 144–62; J. Daniel Hays, *From Every People and Nation: A Biblical Theology of Race* (NSBT; Leicester: Apollos; Downers Grove, IL: InterVarsity Press, 2003), 65–86; Philip F. Elser, "Ezra-Nehemiah as a Narrative of (Re-Invented) Israelite Identity," *BibInt* 11, nos. 3–4 (2003): 413–26; Katherine E.

Ezekiel. Jean-Pierre Ruiz has done a lot of work from a Hispanic perspective on the book of Ezekiel. In his publications he explores the poignancy of living far from one's land and ministering to others in that same situation.[55]

Daniel. The first chapter of this book is particularly interesting. Daniel and his friends—good looking, of stellar character, and bright members of the upper class—are removed from Jerusalem. They are given new names and trained in the many facets of Babylonian learning to serve the empire (1:3–7). The goal is to reprogram them and redefine them culturally and intellectually in the image of the ruling power. In this they excel above all others (1:17–21). But Daniel draws the line at their diet. Scholars wonder if the issue is that this fare includes food offered to another deity, if the problem is that it comes from the king's table, or if their goal just is to follow the dietary laws of Torah.[56]

Whatever the exact reason, a diaspora reading recognizes the symbolism and power of food.[57] Cultural identity (here deeply connected with religious belief) is inseparable from what we eat. How does one know if one is in a Hispanic neighborhood? Look at the restaurants, *pupuserías, taquerías,* and *panaderías!* If you are invited to a Hispanic home, you will be invited to eat. It is not uncommon for Hispanic churches to share meals after services. Food brings us together. And it can lead to a new appreciation of Daniel's convictions.

The prophetic critique of popular religion. It is generally assumed that popular religion in Israel, however defined,[58] was not a good thing in

Southwood, "'And they could not understand Jewish speech': Language, Ethnicity, and Nehemiah's Intermarriage Crisis," *JTS* 62, no. 1 (2011): 1–19.

[55] See Ruiz, *Reading from the Edges,* 71–99. One of the chapters, "An Exile's Baggage: Toward a Postcolonial Reading of Ezekiel," appeared earlier in *Approaching Yehud: New Approaches to the Study of the Persian Period* (ed. J. L. Berquist; SBLSS 50; Atlanta: Society of Biblical Literature, 2007), 117–35. Also note his "Among the Exiles by the River Chebar: A U.S. Hispanic American Reading of Prophetic Cosmology in Ezekiel 1:1–3," *JH/LT* 6, no. 2 (1998): 43–67.

[56] For a convenient list of views, see Ernest Lucas, *Daniel* (Apollos Old Testament Commentary 20; Leicester: Apollos; Downers Grove, IL: InterVarsity Press, 2002), 54–55.

[57] For an awareness of this cultural dynamic, see Norman W. Porteous, *Daniel: A Commentary* (OTL; Philadelphia: Westminster, 1979), 29–32; John E. Goldingay, *Daniel* (WBC 30; Dallas: Word, 1989), 24–25.

[58] For surveys of the data and theories, see Richard S. Hess, *Israelite Religions: An Archaeological and Biblical Survey* (Grand Rapids: Baker Academic,

the prophets' eyes, that it had syncretistic tendencies or aberrant practices. Many Hispanics, however, are Roman Catholic, and for this group
popular religion and its rituals (such as the veneration of *Nuestra Señora
de Guadelupe*) are not necessarily negative. Rather they are an expression of the popular piety and aspirations of a marginalized people, both
in the crossing of borders and in their life here.[59] At the very least, an
appreciation of Hispanic Catholic popular faith can provide insights into
the emotions, ethos, and perspective of ancient religious life and into
how popular religion functions in a community.

Conclusion

Much more could be said, but I close here. I began by citing two factors that today require that multiethnic perspectives be given attention.
On the one hand, the demographic shift in the makeup of Christianity
demands a response and engagement; on the other, the multiple large
diasporas make this call inescapable. These populations are not only
"over there" on another continent; they are also here, within this country
and in our communities.

The second section explained the perspective and convictions of
interpreting with the lens of the Hispanic diaspora, as a particular subset
of this new multiethnic hermeneutical reality. The third section offered
readings of several well-known texts in order to establish the value of
these approaches. This lens can help us all see things in the text that we
may have not noticed before. I have tried to model how diaspora readings treat the text carefully, draw on background work, and utilize other
disciplines, from the social sciences to literature.

I hope to have shown, too, that this is a serious academic exercise,
but it is also more than that. For diaspora communities, these readings

---

2007) and Francesca Stavrakopoulou and John Barton, eds., *Religious Diversity
in Ancient Israel and Judah* (London: T&T Clark, 2010).

[59] Orlando Espín, *The Faith of the People: Theological Reflections on Popu-
lar Catholicism* (Maryknoll, NY: Orbis, 1997); Kathryn Ferguson, Norma A.
Price, and Ted Parks, *Crossing with the Virgin: Stories from the Migrant Trail*
(Tucson: University of Arizona Press, 2010). Also note C. Gilbert Romero,
"Amos 5:21–24: Religion, Politics, and the Latino Experience," *JH/LT* 4, no.
4 (1997): 21–41; "The 'Between Time' as a Basis of Hope: Jeremiah and the
Latino Religious Experience," *Apuntes* 29, no. 1 (2009): 4–17; "The Bible and
the Latino: An Interpretive Dialogue," *Apuntes* 31, no. 1 (2011): 20–36; cf.
Daniel, *Neighbor*, 3–12.

open up the biblical text and allow them to see themselves in its stories and its poetry. *El texto nos acompaña en nuestro perigrinaje de fe* ("the text walks with us in our pilgrimage of faith"). Because the text lives, so can we.

Muchísimas gracias.

For Further Reading

Carroll R., M. Daniel. *Christians at the Border: Immigration, the Church, and the Bible*. Grand Rapids: Baker Academic, 2008.

González, Justo L. *Santa Biblia: The Bible through Hispanic Eyes*. Nashville: Abingdon, 1996.

Nanko-Fernández, Carmen. *Theologizing in Espanglish: Context, Community, and Ministry*. Maryknoll, NY: Orbis, 2010.

Rivera Rodríguez, Luis. "Toward a Diaspora Hermeneutics (Hispanic North America)." Pages 169–89 in *Character Ethics and the Old Testament: Moral Dimensions of Scripture*. Edited by M. Daniel Carroll R. and J. Lapsley. Louisville: Westminster John Knox, 2007.

Ruiz, Jean-Pierre. *Reading from the Edges: The Bible and People on the Move*. Maryknoll, NY: Orbis, 2011.

CHAPTER 2

Response: Multicultural Readings: A Biblical Warrant and an Eschatological Vision

K. K. Yeo

I, too, am grateful to the Institute for Biblical Research for this invitation—not only to be able to respond to Professor Carroll but also to have the opportunity to share a Christian Chinese biblical interpretation.

The brilliant presentation made by Professor Carroll does not need a critical response; I fully empathize with Professor Carroll's work because of who I am. I am an ethnic Chinese born and raised in Malaysia—a multireligious and multiracial country colonized by the British. Malaysia is a land in which Muslims and natives are considered first-class citizens, which means that Chinese Christians are doubly marginalized. I was educated in the United States but taught in Hong Kong for four years before returning to Chicago, where I have taught for the past fifteen years. During the last five years, I have spent more and more time teaching in China, a land that does not allow me to call her "my motherland."

This brief overview of my life will give you an idea of how "migrating" and "mixed up" I am. But except by a matter of degree, who among us is *not* "*mestizo*" and "mobile," to use Professor Carroll's words? Professor Carroll's Hispanic reading brings the issues of hybridity and fluidity *sharply* to our attention, when other cultural lenses may not prove reflective enough.

A Myth and an Authentic Biblical Interpretation

It is a myth in our modern world to assume that one belongs to a pure race, or that one has one simple and unchanging ethnicity, or that one embodies one objective, absolute experience. In biblical

hermeneutics, this myth is exacerbated by the power of sin; it has resulted in biblical interpretations that are partial and idolatrous, and in
theological interpretations that are segregated and subjugating. They
are partial and idolatrous because powerful interpretations claim nor-
mativity, ignoring any requirement to read the Scripture multiculturally.
They also are segregating and subjugating because, at best, the Latinos
can do their own thing and the Koreans theirs; at worst, interpretations
that are marginal continue to cry from the wilderness and apologize for
their readings as "*other* lenses," Chinese-, Hispanic-, African- *hyphenated*
perspectives, while the dominant or assumed normative interpretations
simply claim theirs as Christian or biblical interpretations.

Is it not a matter of difference *in degree only* that the LXX translators,
the author of the Gospel of John, the apostle Paul, Saint Augustine, and
Luther are all doing cultural interpretations of the Bible? In its translation of the Hebrew text, the LXX contemporizes, recreates, and alters
according to Greek cultural lenses. For example, occasional glosses are
added to the text—such as adding moralizing conditions of poor and
rich, good and bad, to the translation of Proverbs (as in 16:7; 15:28a;
19:22). Another example is the way in which embarrassing anthropo-
morphisms are eliminated—such as references to "the mouth of the
Lord" (Josh 9:14) and Moses speaking to the Lord "face to face," or
revising the account of Moses beholding "the glory of the Lord" (Num
12:8) in place of the Hebrew text's usage of God's "form." And, in Isa
65:11, instead of transliterating the ancient Semitic names of the gods
Gad and Meni, the LXX translator updates the text culturally by supply-
ing the names of contemporary gods popular in Hellenized Alexandria:
[Agathos] Daimon and Tyche.[1]

That the LXX translator renders יהוה the name of God in Exod 3:14
from *ehyeh asher ehyeh* ("I am who I am"), and not literally as *ego eimi
ho ego eimi* ("I am who I am")—but to a Greek philosophically-tagged
meaning of *ego eimi ho on* ("I am he who is" or "I am the Existent One" or
simply "I am the Being"), is the case in point.[2] Both "I am" (*ehyeh*) and

---

[1] See Richard Soulen, *Sacred Scripture: A Short History of Interpretation*
(Louisville: Westminster John Knox, 2010).

[2] Note that Aquila and Theodotion translate the name of God as "*esomai
hos esomai*" and "*esomai*" respectively ("I will be who I will be" and "I will be").
For various interpretations and literature, see William H. C. Propp, *Exodus
1–18* (AB 2; New York: Doubleday, 1998), 225; W. R. Arnold, "The Divine
Name in Exodus iii.14," *JBL* 24 (1905): 107–65; E. C. B. MacLaurin, "YHWH:

the tetragrammaton (YHWH יהוה) seem to have derived from *hyh* ("to be" היה *hayah*), which can be translated as "to be," "to become," or even "is-ness."[3] The absolute verb *ehyeh* ("I am") is first-person Qal imperfect of the verb *hyh* ("to be"), a verb rendered in the LXX with a participle functioning as a noun ("I am the being")—thus the Greek language or the Greek philosophical culture of the LXX provides the basis for Philo, Origen, and others to conceive God essentially as the Being.[4] The basic root word of "I am" (and YHWH) does not connote "substance," "pure being," or "essence" but a dynamic, active, living God thundering and acting in human affairs (e.g., God's deliverance of the Israelites in their history). So, which text of Exod 3:14 is more authoritative: the Hebrew or the Greek? Definitely the Hebrew text is authoritative, but also the Greek, is it not? For it is the *ego eimi ho on* translation that allows the Gospel of John and the church fathers to understand the nature of the trinitarian God, an understanding that the Hebrew text does not give clearly. Both texts are authoritative, for only a cross-cultural reading of the Hebrew and Greek of Exod 3:14 gives us an understanding of God that overcomes the limitation of a monocultural reading.

A cross-cultural biblical interpretation allows the biblical texts to exhibit their sacredness, in that Scripture has the power to speak across space and time and to be consequently transforming of the cultures the biblical texts engage with. The Greek and Latin languages and especially the neo-Platonic philosophy serve as the cultural lens for Augustine to express his understanding of Christian theology, and by doing so "re-deem" the Greco-Roman cultures. Frances Young, writing in *Biblical Exegesis and the Formation of Christian Culture*, proves a similar thesis that the New Testament and the Fathers' cross-cultural interpretation of the Bible is profoundly transformative of Western culture:

> The perception that the Jewish scriptures became a substitute set of classics gives us a very different perspective on Christian appropriation [NT and patristics] of this "barbarian" literature. It meant not just their Christological

---

The Origin of the Tetragrammaton," *VT* 12 (1962): 439–63; R. de Vaux, "The Revelation of the Divine Name YHWH," in *Proclamation and Presence* (ed. J. I. Durham and J. R. Porter; Richmond: John Knox, 1970), 48–75; and John I. Durham, *Exodus* (WBC 3; Waco: Word, 1987), 34–41.

[3] See John Courtney Murray, *The Problem of God: Yesterday and Today* (New Haven: Yale University Press, 1964), 7; Durham, *Exodus*, 39.

[4] Andrio König, *Here Am I* (Grand Rapids: Eerdmans, 1982), 67.

interpretation, not simply a supersessionary claim in relation to Jews, but potentially a supersessionary claim in relation to all of ancient culture. With astonishing audacity, a small persecuted community of oddly assorted persons with no natural kinship, no historical identity, claims a universality which challenges the most powerful tradition in ancient society, the Hellenic *paideia* which had taken over the world and colonized other traditions, Latin and Hebrew, Eastern and Western. In the course of this process the very concept of religion was redefined and philosophy reminted. Not only did the Christians prove themselves in the intellectual power struggle, but, to a traditionalist world shaped by unquestioned obligations to a society both human and divine in its constituents (the very word *religio* reflects that element), they introduced the concept of religion as a particular faith-commitment, truth-claim or "-ism" as we understand it.[5]

Likewise, Luther is doing a contextual and cultural reading of "justification by faith through grace" in the context of the social-ecclesial problems faced in Germany then, and his cultural biblical exegesis brought about transformations in Europe. As he used the same lens to read the epistle of James, we now know that it was a misreading (see the works of Luke Timothy Johnson[6] and Elsa Tamez[7]). Clearly, the central theme of Romans is not "justification by faith" but "obedience of faith" (Rom 1:5; 16:26) regarding the gospel of Jesus Christ—an "obedience of faith" that is in sync theologically with James's understanding of "perfect and active faith" (Jas 2:14–26). A critical awareness of cultural identity and presuppositions—one that is common in our contemporary multicultural interpretations—is something we need to apply also to all dominating or normative interpretations, so that biases such as segregations and idolatrous readings can be overcome.

Two Prescriptive Tasks for Multicultural Readings of the Scripture

All theological expression or interpretation is *cross*-cultural to the degree that theology and culture are not identical, although they need

---

[5] Frances Young, *Biblical Exegesis and the Formation of Christian Culture* (Cambridge: Cambridge University Press, 2007), 49 (emphasis added).

[6] Luke Timothy Johnson, *The Letter of James* (AB 37A; New York: Doubleday, 1995), 125–29.

[7] Elsa Tamez, *The Scandalous Message of James: Faith Without Works Is Dead* (New York: Crossroad, 2002).

each other and share some common tasks. If the cultures of the Bible and those of the interpreters are identical, cross-cultural interpretation is not necessary; but if they do not have anything in common, interpretation will not be possible. The need to consider multicultural readings of the Bible is *not* based on trendiness, politically correctness, or competition for powers and recognition. Besides the two factors—demographic shift and forces of globalization—that Professor Carroll mentions, I want to add two *prescriptive* factors for multicultural readings of Scripture:

> One, a biblical warrant for multicultural readings of the Bible as the fulfill-ment of the law (loving one's neighbors); and

> Two, the eschatological drive/vision of the mobile, global church that must be multicultural—as seen in the eschatological Christian worship that is the end of all biblical interpretations.

Multicultural Readings of the Bible as Fulfillment of the Law of Life

To know the biblical warrant for multicultural readings of the Bible is to live a life of discipleship faithful to the text. In other words, multi-cultural reading is neither a luxury nor an option. It is a law of life, a law so important that Jesus equates this law to the law of loving God with all our being. The Gospel writers and Paul—as well as James—reinterpret the fulfillment of the whole Mosaic law in terms of Lev 19:18 (see, e.g., Matt 5:43; 19:19; 22:39; Mark 12:31; 12:33; Luke 10:27; Rom 13:9; Jas 2:8).[8] It is Paul who most beautifully expresses the radical gospel of Jesus as he highlights "loving your neighbor" as the *summation* (or fulfillment)[9] of the Jewish law in Rom 13:8–9, "Leave no debt outstanding, except *the debt to love one another.*" There are two layers of meaning here. First, Paul is saying that we can claim completion and perfection in all other

---

[8] See James Moffatt, *Love in the New Testament* (London: Hodder & Stoughton, 1929); Victor P. Furnish, *The Love Command in the New Testament* (Nashville: Abingdon, 1972); Pheme Perkins, *Love Commands in the New Testa-ment* (New York: Paulist, 1982); Viktor Warnach, *Agape: Die Liebe als Grund-motiv der neutestamentlichen Theologie* (Düsseldorf: Patmos-Verlag, 1951); Ceslaus Spicq, *Agapè dans le Nouveau Testament: Analyse des Textes* (3 vols.; Paris: Libraire Lecoffre, 1958–1959); Paul Brett, *Love Your Neighbor: The Bible as Christian Ethics Today* (London: Darton, Longman & Todd, 1992).

[9] Romans 13:9 is a summation of the Ten Commandments (Rom 13:10 says "love is the fulfillment of the law" [author's translation]; see also Jas 2:8, the "royal law" as loving one's neighbor).

religious duties except in the command to love. Second, without loving others, one will not become fully human. In other words, it is *in the mutually loving process of paying the eternal debt of love that we are fulfilling each other's humanity.* Thus, multicultural readings of Scripture are essential because of the theological anthropology assumed by the law of life of "loving our neighbors." Monocultural reading is self-limiting and self-destructive because it makes an idol out of the meaning of the sacred text.

It would be dishonest not to disclose to you the cultural lens I use to read the Pauline anthropology in Rom 13:9 that way.[10] This lens, I believe, is closer to the Hebraic anthropological understanding than a Greek anthropology, but neither has come up with the kind of linguistic and cultural complexity that Confucianist discourse has. The Confucian language of 仁 (**ren**) and 仁人 (**ren**ren)[11] can amplify the text of Rom 13:9. The word 仁 (**ren**), used to translate the Greek word *agapē* in the Chinese Bible, is used no fewer than eighty times in the *Analects* and can be translated

---

[10] For more on this reading, see K. K. Yeo, *Musing with Confucius and Paul: Toward a Chinese Christian Theology* (Eugene, OR: Cascade, 2008).

[11] Readers need to note that the English transliteration *ren* can refer to two different Chinese words, 仁 (**ren**) and 人 (*ren*), meaning "humaneness" and "person" respectively. Here we are discussing the first word 仁; thus I use bold type to differentiate this word from the other word (meaning "person"). When the two words appear together, the order is always 仁人 (**ren**ren), meaning "humane person" or "benevolent person." Chinese does not have articles, and the word itself does not indicate singular or plural. In *Analects* 12:22, **ren** is equated with benevolence (for fellow human beings). **Ren**ren can mean a humane person or humane persons.

I will note the source of the English translation of the *Analects* used or mention if it is my translation. The citation of the *Analects* in Chinese scholarship gives the title of the book or chapter without the numbering of the verse. However, the citation of the *Analects* in non-Chinese scholarship often gives the precise numbering of passages from the *Analects*. The problem is that the numbering of passages from the *Analects* is not always the same in different editions. For the English citation of the *Analects* in this chapter, I will follow the numbering of Lau or Li or Ames and Rosemont, indicating them as, e.g., "1:3" and noting which source I use. As for the major Chinese commentaries on the *Analects*, I use He Yan and Xing Bing, *Lunyu Zhushu* [*Commentary of the Analects*] (Beijing: Peking University Press, 1999); Yang Bojun, *Lunyu Yizhu* [*Commentary of the Analects*] (Taipei: Wunan, 1992); Qian Mu, *Lunyu Xinjie* [*The Analects: New Interpretation*] (Taipei, Taiwan: Dongda, 2003); Jin Liangnian, *Lunyu Yizhu* [*Commentary of the Analects*] (Shanghai: Shanghai Guji, 2006); Li Ling, *Sangjiaguo: Wodou Lunyu* [*Homeless Dog: My Reading of the Analects*] (Taiyuan: Shanxi Renmin, 2007).

as benevolence (Lau)[12] or humanness (Waley)[13] or the kind of love that is empathetic 忠 (*zhong*) and reciprocal 恕 (*shu, Analects* 4:15).[14] Even the two ideograms of this Chinese word ("person" [人 (*ren*)] connotes self or a human being, and "two" [二 (*er*)] connotes relation)[15] symbolizes human-relatedness. In the Confucian interpersonal ethic, he teaches that "in order to establish oneself, one must establish others" (*Analects* 6:30).[16] In other words, to be truly human is to be responsible *to* and *for* others (*Analects* 6:13). The interpersonal relationships one has within a community and the acts one does for others constitute together the essence of humanity. To be *ren* ("humanness"), to be benevolent or compassionate, is to be in relationship, to be interdependent.

Benevolence or humaneness is universally cherished—whether it is expressed culturally as *ren* or *agapē* by Confucius and Paul respectively. Of course, Confucian *ren* and Pauline *agapē* are not the same; one is concerned with love extended from the family to others within a structured society, and the other is concerned with the self-sacrificing love for others that extends to the family of God.[17] Nevertheless, for Confucius *and* Paul,

---

[12] Lau, *Analects, passim*. Other translations are "human-heartedness" (E. R. Hughes), "humanity," "virtue" (H. G. Creel), "human-relatedness," "charity," "humanity" (W. T. Chan), "morality," "compassion" (Lin Yutang), "human-to-humanness" (F. S. C. Northrop). Cf. Fung Yulan, *A Short History of Chinese Philosophy* (ed. Derk Bodde; New York: Macmillan, 1948), 69–73; Yang Bojun, *Lunyu Yizhu*, 18–21, 221; Chan Wing-tsit, "Chinese and Western Interpretations of *Ren* (Humanity)," *JOCP* 2 (1975): 108–9.

[13] Arthur Waley, *The Analects of Confucius* (New York: Vintage, 1989), *passim*; Raymond Dawson, trans., *Confucius: The Analects* (Oxford: Oxford University Press, 1993), *passim*; Edward Slingerland, trans., *Confucius Analects with Selections from Traditional Commentaries* (Indianapolis: Hackett, 2003), 238, translate *ren* as "goodness."

[14] In *Analects* 12:22, when asked by Fan Chi the meaning of *ren*, Confucius replied that *ren* is to love people 愛人 (*airen*). *Ren* is not just loving one's fellow beings (12:22).

[15] Tu Weiming says, "Etymologically *ren* consists of two parts, one a simple ideogram of a human figure, meaning the self, and the other with two horizontal strokes, suggesting human relations" (*Confucian Thought: Selfhood as Creative Transformation* [Albany, NY: State University of New York Press, 1985], 84).

[16] Author's translation. See Qian Mu, *Lunyu Xinjie*, 224; Yang Bojun, *Lunyu Yizhu*, 141–42.

[17] Paul and Confucius have different understandings of loving others. They have different explanations of the source and content of love. The comparison between Confucius and Paul may be unfair, as Confucius did not know Christ,

the law of life is "to love others" (Rom 13:8–9; *Analects* 15:9 **ren**ren are "not saving their own lives but sacrificing them in order to perfect the virtue of benevolence"). Both **ren** (benevolence toward others) and *agapē* (divine love) are *reciprocal*, but *agapē* is unconditional. *Agapē* as shown in the cruciform love does not demand of the other the satisfaction of one's own needs. **Ren**, as love, does acknowledge mutual indebtedness as the basic human condition; cruciform love, however, does not require reciprocity of reward or repayment. For Chinese readers of the Bible, a cross-cultural reading of Rom 13:9 inevitably evokes the creative meaning of *cruciform ren*—that is, a self-critical cultural reading that emphasizes extending one's self-sacrificing love toward one's enemies and not manipulating others in order to achieve one's ends. And I hope—for *all* readers of the Bible—this *cruciform ren* serves as the alternative ethic of community formation in the Roman Empire, or any place in our world today, even more so in our multicultural readings of the Bible. Thus, the biblical imperative of doing cross-cultural reading is not simply to read the Bible culturally, but more significantly, to read the culture biblically.

The Eschatological Vision of the Global Church That Is to Be Multicultural

The Bible has no sacred language, and Christianity has no sacred culture; the gospel of the church is neither culture- nor language-specific. As Lamin Sanneh writes, Christianity from its beginning until now has

---

and Paul did. Confucius may have believed that *tian* ("heaven") imparted *ren* ("love") as part of human nature 性 (*xing*), but he did not know of the cruciform love of God as shown on the cross. Paul knows of love among people, and he traces the source of that love to God. God has demonstrated that love by sacrificing his only begotten Son on the cross for the salvation of the world. Paul's understanding of the passion of Christ as the love of God can be used to supplement Confucius's understanding of *ren* ("love"), which has the tendency to be practiced limitedly in a family or clan context. The different ways of extending love in Confucian and Pauline ethics can be traced to their different understandings of heaven 天 (*tian*) and God (*Theos*). Confucius lacks Paul's understanding of the personhood of God; the move forward for Confucius is not toward God but toward full humanity, i.e., to creatively fulfill the mandate of heaven by being *renren* ("a benevolent person"). To become a benevolent or humane person, one must follow the established norms, rites 禮 (*li*), and way 道 (*dao*), and one must be moral (*de*) and love 愛 (*ai*) others. If "one observes the rites and rituals and overcomes oneself, one will be benevolent" (*Analects* 12:1, author's translation).

been "a translated religion without a revealed language."[18] The biblical message is always proclaimed "*in-carnationally*," that is, in its own culture "*in-linguistically*." We should take our cue from Pentecost, where the gospel is presented in the local tongues of the people (Acts 2:1–13). It is the biblical paradigm that warrants us to take local language and homegrown interpretation seriously, for we have seen in church history that when theology is not translated into local tongues, neither is the culture transformed (or fulfilled), nor does Scripture maintain its sacred force to transform lives.

The mission of the global church is not simply to ride on the global forces, but more importantly, to empower and mobilize the local churches in the matrix of diversity in unity. The global church is multicultural. According to Acts, God's blessing and revelation of his work is impartial (10:34–35), especially in the worldwide geographical and cultural diversity of the early Christian movement, from Jerusalem to Caesarea, Antioch, Turkey, Greece, Rome, Spain . . . and many other places not yet on our radar screen. *God sees no boundaries, and truth does not respect borders.* The Bible does not speak of the Jews as the only or only true people of God; in fact, the Bible constantly wants to use a hybridized figure to redefine the source. Paul uses Abraham as the father of both Jews and Gentiles—that is, *all* who have faith (Rom 4:16). Luke traces Adam as the Son of God in the genealogy of Jesus because Adam, the Son of God, represents all human beings.

There is much to be said about cultural diversity as a gift of God to humankind—especially the church. Thus finding the complement of others is a mutually rewarding process as human beings and a church. Almost countless kinds of sea creatures and animals and plants are created, according to Gen 1, and God affirms the goodness of his work of diversity and beauty. The creation of the human race, people groups (nations, see Gen 10; 17), and God's blessing of different languages (Acts 2:4) and cultural practices (Dan 7:14) are seen *as* reflections of God's *glory*. This glory of God is manifested in various tongues, different musical instruments, and diverse styles of worship; thus the global church is envisioned in Revelation as complementary in diversity: "there was a great multitude that no one could count, from *every* nation, from *all* tribes and peoples and languages, standing before the throne and before

---

[18] Lamin Sanneh, *Whose Religion Is Christianity? The Gospel Beyond the West* (Grand Rapids: Eerdmans, 2003), 97.

the Lamb, robed in white, with palm branches in their hands" (Rev 7:9; see also 5:9; 14:6). In order to see cultural diversity as a gift, each culture has to take an outward step and journey to the others, and this is especially true in biblical interpretations that seek to overcome suspicion and fear with respect and trust.

I assume that none of us, as Bible interpreters, seeks a level playing field. We are all *different,* therefore *uniquely gifted* by God as "the others" who have the potential to contribute to the whole of humanity and the vitality of the global church. It is part and parcel of this aesthetic teleology/purpose of God's redemption of the cosmos, whereby the matrix of diversity in unity runs through the biblical narrative of creation and redemption. In the cosmic church of the *eschaton,* none is underprivileged, none is at the center, but all are drawn to Christ and fully redeemed by him. We will all be around the throne and the banquet table, when "every tribe and language and people and nation" glorify God (Rev 5:9; 7:9; 14:6) who alone is absolute and sovereign, the wholly Other (the Alpha and the Omega), and yet the Lamb of God who is fully human and fully divine. Is it not this narrative of Jesus Christ that provides the clarity of the Abraham and the Ruth narratives of alienation and migration? Therefore, this christocentric narrative is what also links and redeems the Hispanic, the Chinese, the African, the Jews, the Palestinians, of loss and pain.

Conclusion

Multicultural reading of the biblical text is geared toward a global biblical interpretation whose theological ethics is that of loving one's neighbor. This is a virtue of humility and an ethic of shared responsibility since any cultural interpretation—whether Hispanic or English—needs the theology of eschatological critique.[19] That is, Christ who is truly divine and truly human discloses the eschatological dawning of God's truth and signals the limitation of interpreters' present knowledge. While every indigenous theology may be valid in its own context, every theology is partial—and therefore, its limitations can be overcome through cross-cultural, global interpretations.

---

[19] K. K. Yeo, "Culture and Intersubjectivity as Criteria for Negotiating Meanings in Cross-Cultural Interpretations," in *The Meaning We Choose: Hermeneutical Ethics, Indeterminacy, and the Conflict of Interpretations* (ed. Charles Cosgrove; LBH/OTS 411; London: T&T Clark, 2004), 81, 99.

For Further Reading

Ames, Roger T., and Henry Rosemont, Jr. *The Analects of Confucius: A Philosophical Translation.* New York: Ballentine, 1999.

Confucius. *The Analects.* Translated by D. C. Lau. New York: Penguin, 1979

Cosgrove, Charles, Harold Weiss, and K. K. Yeo. *Cross-Cultural Paul: Journeys to Others, Journeys to Ourselves.* Grand Rapids: Eerdmans, 2005.

He Guanghu, and Daniel H. N. Yeung, eds. *Sino-Christian Theology Reader.* 2 vols. Hong Kong: Institute of Sino-Christian Studies, 2009.

Patte, Daniel, ed. *The Global Biblical Commentary.* Nashville: Abingdon, 2004.

Winter, Ralph D., and Steven C. Hawthorne, eds. *Perspectives on the World Christian Movement: A Reader.* 4th ed. Pasadena: William Carey Library, 2009.

Yeo, K. K. *What Has Jerusalem to Do with Beijing? Biblical Interpretation from a Chinese Perspective.* Harrisburg, PA: Trinity Press International, 1998.

CHAPTER 3

Neither Tamil Nor Sinhalese: Reading Galatians with Sri Lankan Christians

David A. deSilva

It has become a truism that one's social location shapes one's ability to see what is in a text and to hear what that text is challenging one's community and oneself to desire, to do, and to become.[1] Social location both opens up possibilities for engaging a text and limits the possibilities for engagement: the lenses cast over our eyes by our social location, its ideologies, and its interests threaten to eclipse facets of the text, especially at those points where Scripture would most challenge the ideologies and interests that drive the society in which we have been nurtured. A reading informed by conversations about the text from multiple social

---

[1] The role of social location in biblical hermeneutics has been an area of significant investment and productivity in recent decades. See, e.g., the seminal works by R. S. Sugirtharajah, ed., *Voices from the Margin: Interpreting the Bible in the Third World* (Maryknoll, NY: Orbis, 1991); idem, *The Postcolonial Bible* (Sheffield: Sheffield Academic Press, 1998); idem, *Postcolonial Criticism and Biblical Interpretation* (Oxford: Oxford University Press, 2002); idem, *Postcolonial Reconfigurations: An Alternative Way of Reading the Bible and Doing Theology* (St. Louis: Chalice, 2003); Cain Hope Felder, ed., *Stony the Road We Trod: African American Biblical Interpretation* (Minneapolis: Augsburg Fortress, 1991); John R. Levison and Priscilla Pope-Levison, *Jesus in Global Contexts* (Louisville: Westminster John Knox, 1992); Fernando F. Segovia and Mary Ann Tolbert, eds., *Reading from This Place* (Minneapolis: Fortress, 1995); Fernando F. Segovia, *Decolonizing Biblical Studies: A View from the Margins* (Maryknoll, NY: Orbis, 2000); Musa W. Dube, *Postcolonial Feminist Interpretation of the Bible* (St. Louis: Chalice, 2000); Randall C. Bailey, ed., *Yet with a Steady Beat: Contemporary U.S. Afrocentric Biblical Interpretation* (Semeia 42; Atlanta: Society of Biblical Literature, 2003); Daniel Patte, ed., *The Global Bible Commentary* (Nashville: Abingdon, 2004).

locations, by contrast, allows us to triangulate beyond the blinders of our own social location, to see much more of the vision for discipleship and life together in the text, to hear more clearly its challenge to us within our social location (hence, its fuller relevance to us).

In our models for exegesis, we typically nurture a reading from at least one other important social location: in regard to Galatians, this would be the location of Paul and his Galatian Christian converts. Solid historical exegesis is an exercise in cross-cultural hermeneutics. We are trying to hear a text within a profoundly different culture (first-century Mediterranean, generally northeastern Mediterranean culture) with a political system, political ideology, economics, social institutions, and religious culture profoundly different from our own. I strenuously reject the easy identification of sociohistorical exegesis as "Eurocentric":[2] it is, rather, cross-cultural. And most of these early Christian texts are addressing people in locations that are clearly not European (Syria, various provinces in what is now Turkey), and certainly not people who are dominant-cultural Europeans even when they are in Macedonia, Greece, or Rome.

We have come to appreciate more and more the value also of engaging readings from other, modern social locations—of learning what our sisters and brothers in Christ in other places in the world are seeing and wrestling with as they engage the Scriptures, and particularly when they engage the Scriptures also in conversation with the original, historical social location of its author and audience. Incorporating both historical *and* global perspectives on biblical interpretation provides a level of triangulation that nurtures a reading and interpretation that is as fully informed by multiple social locations and thus as little hampered by the lenses of a single social location as possible. Reading from three locations, each reading from one's own location is challenged, refined, expanded. We realize, both from listening to one another across the room and from listening to Paul across the millennia that the text is addressing questions that we did not ask and challenging ideological assumptions that we did not question.

---

[2] As, e.g., in William D. Myers's equation of the practice of source, form, and redaction criticism with "the Eurocentric approach" ("The Hermeneutical Dilemma of the African-American Biblical Student," in *Stony the Road We Trod: African American Biblical Interpretation* [ed. Cain H. Felder; Minneapolis: Augsburg Fortress, 1991], 43 [40–56]).

In this essay, I will report on several conversations from around the table in Colombo Theological Seminary and around other tables in Colombo regarding how Galatians, and our attempts to hear Galatians in its historical, pastoral context, opened up avenues for the critical examination of the situation of Sri Lankan churches among those present. It is my hope that hearing these conversations now in our Western context may help us both to think more fully about Galatians' word to us *and* to reflect on the nature of, and means of enacting, our partnership with Christians in a very different cultural and social setting.

Dialogue with the Dominant Religion

Sri Lankan Christians could relate to Paul's audience and the tensions reflected in the Galatian situation in some ways much more closely than my students in Ohio. In Sri Lanka, Christianity is a minority religion. Buddhism is the majority religion, claiming the loyalty of about 70 percent of the island's inhabitants, with Hinduism a distant second, claiming 15 percent of the population as adherents.[3] Adherence to these religions divides rather sharply along ethnic lines, with the Sinhalese population aligning chiefly with Buddhism and the Tamil population with Hinduism. Muslims and Christians each account for about 7 percent of the population, with adherents from both ethnic groups, as well as descendants of Arab traders and colonizing races. Also in a manner much more reflecting the first-century situation, almost everyone *does* claim to follow a particular religious practice.

The presence of Buddhism, the religion of the political leaders, is overwhelming; the promotion of Buddhism as a focus of political and social unity is also quite striking. For example, shortly after the decisive assault on the Liberation Tigers of Tamil Eelam, President Rajapakse erected statues of the Buddha throughout the north and east of the island as a celebration of the reunification of the country, despite the fact that the majority of the Tamil Hindu population lives in those regions. It should therefore not have surprised me to find that dialogue with Buddhism—the religion from which many Christians had emerged, and

---

[3] These statistics differ somewhat from the last official census taken in 2001, available at www.statistics.gov.lk. That census did not include the Northern, Batticaloa, and Trincomalee districts on account of the civil unrest, and therefore did not reflect the full extent of the Hindu population.

the religion still followed by many of a convert's family members, neighbors, and governing officials—would be a point of recurring interest for Sri Lankan readers of Galatians.

Finding constructive bridges between the Christian gospel and the Buddhist Dhamma is an area of great concern so that Christian converts can articulate their faith in a way that shows respect for, and ongoing engagement with, the Buddhist heritage shared by so many outside the church. Such engagement could also help allay the fear of non-Christians that converts to Christianity from Buddhism are (or will become) opponents of Buddhism and agents of Western imperialism. There was great interest in Paul's model of passing from the tutelage of the "pedagogue" (Gal 3:23–25), or of multiple guardians and stewards (4:2–3), into the state of being mature heirs in the household of God as a model by which Sri Lankan Christians coming from Buddhist backgrounds might look back constructively upon their Buddhist heritage and even integrate it into their Christian worldview.[4] While our exegesis of Galatians tended in the direction of suggesting that Paul is quite negative about the quality of life under the pedagogue (who is more of an authoritarian babysitter than a tutor),[5] the early church nurtured a strong tradition of *preparatio evangelica* that would encourage Sri Lankan Christians to engage their former cultural and religious traditions as contributing positively to their formation and their readiness to embrace the gospel. In this way, Sri Lankan Christians are invited to engage the Buddha and his teachings not as the rejected other but as the mentor whose formative work in the disciple must be completed by another Master, integrating their past religious experience and formation into their new formation in Christ. As Prabo Mihindukulasuriya commented on this point, "If the Greek and Latin Fathers could express gratitude to God for the wealth of their Pagan heritage, Christians of Buddhist culture can celebrate with at least as much enthusiasm. For surely, the discerning enjoyment of

---

[4] Prabo Mihindukulasuriya, "Without Christ I Could Not Be a Buddhist: An Evangelical Response to Christian Self-Understanding in a Buddhist Context," *Journal of the Colombo Theological Seminary* 6 (2010): 83–110. The material on Gal 4:8–9 appears on pp. 102–4.

[5] Thus N. H. Young, "*Paidogogos*: The Social Setting of a Pauline Metaphor," *NovT* 29 (1987): 150–76, esp. 157–65; Richard N. Longenecker, "The Pedagogical Nature of the Law in Galatians 3:19–4:7," *JETS* 25 (1982): 53–61, esp. 53–56; David A. deSilva, *Global Readings: A Sri Lankan Commentary on Paul's Letter to the Galatians* (Eugene, OR: Cascade, 2011), 180–82.

the wealth of Buddhism is part of the 'all things' for which Christ has matured and entitled us."[6]

For but one example: The Buddha had identified desire, "the entangling and embroiling craving," as the worm at the heart of human existence, the thing most to be eliminated (*Dhammapada* 180, 359).[7] Paul's diagnosis is quite similar, locating the essential source of suffering and distress in "desires," specifically those that "spring from the 'flesh,'" which, when acted upon, produce the vices listed as "works of the flesh" (Gal 5:19–21). The Buddha would have read Paul's list with approval, for he had previously identified as "fetters" to be renounced or uprooted many of the same inner-personal and interpersonal manifestations of self-centered desire, including anger, pride, jealousy, selfishness, deceit, hatred, lust, and hypocrisy (*Dhammapada* 7, 221, 262–263, 407). The Buddha nourished both the commitment and the discipline required to destroy these "cankers," so that the individual "whose senses are subdued like horses well trained by a charioteer" might be characterized by patience, freedom from anger, and self-control, which are the marks of the true "holy person" (*Dhammapada* 93–95, 399–400). The person who is fully formed in the Spirit and its fruit (Gal 5:22–24), who has put the passions to death, would manifest many of the characteristics prized in the Buddha's vision of the *arahat*.

One of the most significant differences between Paul's vision and the Buddha's is the role of the divine in assisting the disciple. The Buddha taught reliance on oneself and one's discipline to overcome desire; Paul proclaims the personal interest and investment of the divine in empowering human beings to overcome the desires that produce personal, interpersonal, and societal suffering. God's gift of the Holy Spirit is the means by which to find freedom from the power of desire (as well as anger and delusion) so as to love fully and in a truly other-centered way. It is precisely at this point that those who have experienced life in Christ may be able to say, with respect, that they have come to know and experience what the Buddha did not. Like Virgil in Dante's *Divine Comedy*, the Buddha can guide a person only so far, after which it must fall to someone who has experienced that life of the Spirit that Virgil (or the Buddha) had not shared. The cross of Jesus Christ continues thus

---

[6] Mihindukulasuriya, "Without Christ," 103–4.

[7] Translations are from Acharya Buddharakkhita, trans., *The Dhammapada: The Buddha's Path of Wisdom* (Kandy: Buddhist Publication Society, 1985).

to present a "stumbling block" to Sri Lankan Buddhists in regard to its rejection of self-reliance, teaching reliance on the power and guidance of God's Spirit instead. Nevertheless, it is also interpreted as the remedy for the very situation that the Buddha accurately diagnosed.

When All Are Clothed in Christ

Two passages especially captured the attention and stimulated the contextual analysis of the Sri Lankans with whom I dialogued. These were, perhaps predictably, Gal 3:26–29 and, perhaps not so predictably, Gal 4:1–11. Although they were reluctant to talk about ethnic tensions at first, no doubt because there were both Tamil and Sinhalese Christians present and it is understandably a threatening topic to introduce into such a room, once the foreigner brought it up, it unleashed wave after wave of conversation and analysis of the extent to which Christians dealt with healthfully or perpetuated this particular "dividing wall of hostility" and the role of the church in Sri Lanka in nurturing reconciliation. My conversation partners, however, were quick to add the dimensions of gender and caste or class to the conversation, bearing witness to the necessity of dealing with all manner of division and power differentials together as part of a problematic web that the gospel challenges as a whole.

In his vision for the new creation, and hence for life in the church, Paul declares that the divisions and hierarchies created by the constructions of "Jew and Greek," "slave and free," and "male and female" are transcended in the church, where all are clothed anew with Christ and thus share in the unity of the one Person who now lives in them. In this new act of creation, the dividing walls of ethnicity are torn down, social prejudices are neutralized, and gender inequalities and male chauvinism are negated. These barriers continue to divide and subordinate people across the landscape of Sri Lankan society. The importance of ethnic and religious identity, generally in the combinations of Sinhalese Buddhists on the one hand and Tamil Hindus on the other, undermines any sense even of national identity as Sri Lankans. These lines have been more deeply etched by three decades of civil war and by lingering prejudice and inequities across these particular divides. Socioeconomic divisions between rich and poor are also sharp and glaring. The caste system, which is closely linked to one's ethnicity, still exercises power in Sri Lankan social relationships, particularly in rural areas. Lines of gender inequality also pervade Sri Lankan society, again manifested more strongly in the rural areas and villages, where the woman alone may take on the role of the servant on the road, in the dining room, and even in the bedchamber.

In this conversation, the focus kept coming back to the practice of the church: does Christian practice perpetuate these divisions and the social inequalities they inscribe, or does Christian practice challenge them, witnessing to the "new humanity" being formed in Christ in their communities, where Christ is all and in all? To what extent do we ignore the garment of Christ draped around each one of us, peering again under another's robe to see and treat that person according to the old garments of this world's divisions?

There was much to celebrate, and much to continue to strive after. A number of Christian churches held, and continue to hold, bilingual services in Tamil and Sinhalese, bringing members of both major ethnic groups together in worship and around a shared communion table. In this setting, they were able to practice the command to "welcome one another as Christ welcomed us" (Rom 15:7) and provided a valuable witness particularly during the decades of the civil war to the power of Christ and the Holy Spirit to reconcile people one to another. This witness continues where churches give intentional thought to bringing Christians from both ethnic groups together, nurturing an environment of mutual acceptance, honor, and partnership in mission in Sri Lanka (even if fully bilingual or trilingual services are more sporadic).

Latent ethnic divisions still surface, however, when two young people in the church, one Tamil and one Sinhalese, begin to think seriously about marriage, a union that even Christian parents might resist. Similarly, the prejudicial structures of the caste system surface in the church when it comes to children marrying. Even Christian leaders have objected to their son or daughter marrying a person from a different caste or ethnic background, such that the old dividing lines trump oneness in Christ. It was encouraging, however, that a growing number of Christian parents are blessing marriages between children of different ethnic communities, heralding the church's increasingly healing influence on the nation. That young people who formerly harbored racial prejudice before coming to Christ have experienced transformation and gone on to marry partners of a different race or caste is also evidence of this.

The socially prescribed lines of inequality in gender roles can intrude upon Christian homes, with the husband still taking his superior role for granted. Domestic violence is sadly not uncommon. Often pastors have to deal with couples where the husband has used violence to enforce his supposed authority. There was increasing agreement, however, that the expectations that relegate females to a supporting role at best, and often to an inferior status, are not inherent in creation but rather in the fall and the curse (see Gen 3:16c), and thus not a continuing part of the new creation. This increasingly extends into the larger life of the Christian community (except in the more fundamentalist sects), where one's immersion into Christ and one's responsiveness to the Holy Spirit—and not one's gender—guide how one will contribute, and be valued as a contributor, to the life of the church. My conversation partners were particularly aware of the church's call to witness, in the midst of a society divided along ethnic and caste lines, to the power of God's Spirit and the reality of God's plan to reconcile all things in God's Son.

I need to give some mention here to the importance of the Antioch incident and its implications for these readers (Gal 2:11–14). They voiced strong concern over the fact that the communion table remains the most blatant place of violation of "the truth of the gospel" as Paul sought to defend it in Antioch. They criticized the practice of some churches of restricting access to the communion table to those who belong to its particular denomination, excluding others who have made the same commitment to follow Jesus and received the same Spirit. Paul would challenge the posture of saying that "our mutual reliance on Jesus is not sufficient for sharing together at the table, though perhaps if you would do the things that would make you more like us, then we could receive communion together." Or, in the case of the historic splits within the church, it is no longer the case that one stream can say to another with integrity, "You are always welcome to share in communion with us, provided you come back into our fold." Paul would hear this as just another echo of the invitation that might have issued forth from the Jewish Christian table in Antioch (Gal 2:11–14)—the sort of invitation that the Judaizers would eventually extend. It was especially vital for these Christians that churches structure their congregational and intercongregational life in such a way that would bring Tamil and Sinhalese together, and that sharing at a common table was more than worth the hassles of bilingual and even trilingual services at least once each month.

Denominationalism is itself a complex problem in the context of Sri Lanka. Despite being a small minority on the island, the Christian church still makes room for all the diversity and divisions that one finds in countries where Christianity (especially Protestant Christianity, with its tendency toward fragmentation) has been the majority religion for centuries. This phenomenon is, in part, a product of Western missionary practice both during the long history of colonialism and in the postcolonial setting, with Western Christian groups seeking to replicate their particular brand of Christianity in Sri Lanka. In effect, we missionize in the same way that corporations globalize: we go to set up a McDonald's, Burger King, or Wendy's, rather than working together to sell hamburgers, even though the multiplicity of denominational bodies is itself a detriment to Christian witness and presence in Sri Lanka, giving the non-Christian majority there the opportunity to shame Sri Lankan Christians for their lack of cohesiveness and their lack of clarity and agreement concerning the faith and religious practice for which they are leaving behind their ancestral religions and breaking with their neighbors. Of course, new splits also happen within Sri Lankan churches, and yet new denominations unto themselves spring up, often because of the personal interests of one or more leaders.

In the face of this phenomenon, my conversation partners were sensitive to the need for their churches and other churches to focus on what binds different Christian groups together and to work more closely together and cease to function as an array of Western cults in competition with one another. Their Buddhist, Hindu, and Muslim neighbors do not need to hear from one church what other Christians have gotten wrong but they themselves have gotten right. The churches need instead to provide a unified witness if they are to give their neighbors in Sri Lanka a testimony that they can trust and will have to take seriously.

The *Stoicheia* in Sri Lanka

Paul's discussion of the unfolding story of God's dealing with people before and after the death of Jesus prompted conversations about where Sri Lankan Christians fit in to Paul's scheme and the implications of the same for their analysis of their context. In particular, there was a great deal of interest in reflecting together about what Paul might have identified as the *stoicheia* operative in Sri Lanka, against whose ongoing governing and limiting influence Christians need to be on guard.

It is still not entirely clear what Paul had in mind when he spoke of the *stoicheia tou kosmou*, but the range of what his audience would have

understood by this phrase is fairly narrow.[8] The *stoicheia* are, in some
sense, spiritual or cosmic (e.g., astral or elemental) forces exercising authority over the human race. They represent the power of the basic principles of a society's way of ordering reality and doing things, into which
we are socialized from our birth into a social group.[9] This socialization
limits the options we perceive for our responses, our relationships, even
our ambitions. Paul insightfully described our condition as human beings in society as a kind of slavery, or as that of children under various
disciplinarians and guardians (Gal 4:1–11).

My conversation partners were quick to identify *stoicheia* in their
setting, beginning with the belief that astral bodies exercise beneficent or
malign influence on human life, and hence the use of horoscopes and astrology to determine auspicious times for particular undertakings (their
first association with "observing days and months and seasons and years"),
planning weddings, funerals, even business appointments accordingly.
They analyzed their socialization and ongoing setting from the perspective of inquiring into "what ways of thinking, values, sociopolitical categories and systems are deeply ingrained in our culture and our logic and
practice, pulling counter to the direction of the 'new creation.'"

Their short list included the ideology of ethnicity and its effect
on forming personal identity and regulating relationships; the bond
between Buddhism and nationalism; the overemphasis on education,
especially in cities, by which children are driven to excel, valuing success more than life, practicing competition for a limited good (seats in
university) as a primary mode of social interaction, rather than coop-
eration with a view to expanding access to this good; the ideology of
patriarchy, according to which gender is determinative for a person's
potential, value, role, and access to power in every sphere, domestic,
social, and political; the ideology of militarism, with its belief that
violence can produce peace, and the corollary that the suppression of
resistance means that concerns regarding justice and peace have been

---

[8] See, further, Josef Blinzler, "Lexicalisches zu dem Terminus *ta stoicheia tou kosmou*," in *Studiorum Paulinorum Congressus Internationalis Catholicus II* (Rome: Pontifical Institute, 1963), 427–43; D. Rusam, "Neue Belege zu dem *stoicheia tou kosmou* (Gal 4,3.9; Kol 2,8.20)," *ZNW* 83 (1992): 119–25; J. Louis Martyn, *Galatians* (AB 33A; New York: Doubleday, 1997), 395; deSilva, *Global Readings*, 198–201.

[9] G. B. Caird, *Principalities and Powers* (Oxford: Oxford University Press, 1956), 51.

addressed; the belief in karma-samsara, which also places responsibility for poverty, suffering, and pain on the individual, who pays for the lack of merit of a past incarnation, relieving, in turn, those who witness poverty, suffering, or pain of the responsibility to help, and sparing the social structures much-needed scrutiny in regard to the systemic problems and failures that perpetuate poverty and suffering among part of the population.

As residents of a developing country that has also spent centuries as a colony of a Western power (quite literally under "custodians and guardians" in the form of the Portuguese, then the Dutch, then the British), and more recently as part of the globalization of corporations and business, these readers also named Westernization as a powerful *stoicheion* to be examined. The formerly colonized continue to act out the script that the colonizers had pressed upon them: "look to us, imitate us, what we have is good, what we have is better than what you can gain by following your own path." Of course, this tendency is exacerbated by Western Christians (and their publishers and promoters) who market their goods to the global church as the answers to the challenges of every situation and setting. It is also possible that Sri Lankan Christians seek to imitate their Western sisters and brothers as a way to transcend their minority status in Sri Lanka by identifying more clearly with a culture that is dominant in large and empowered countries elsewhere.

The Western appearance—and, in some ways, the Western *ethos*—of Sri Lankan Christianity is another stumbling block to its acceptance in postcolonial Sri Lanka, at a time when leaders and educators are trying to help form a truly Sri Lankan identity and culture. In a sense, the postcolonial climate appears to have helped some Sri Lankan Christians, at least, become much more carefully attuned to the issue of Westernization in the church. My Sri Lankan conversation partners kept coming back to this topic as a facet of their situation most akin to the dynamics of Judaizing in the Galatians' setting from a cultural and political perspective, though without the theological weight of Judaizing.

Sri Lankan Christians continue to live within a largely colonized Christianity. Even when services are offered in Sinhala, for example, the music is often a Sinhalese translation of a Western hymn or praise song, sung in Western fashion with Western instruments. Sri Lankan churches have to contend with undesirable Western imports such as the prosperity gospel, seeking to exchange the Christian gospel of transformation into the likeness of the self-giving and obedient Jesus into the expectation that God will give Christians worldwide access to the American dream. Some Sri Lankan Christians have bought into King James Bible only-ism, an astounding triumph for colonialism in the church. A translation made in the land and in the language of the British colonizers is promoted in some Sri Lankan Christian circles as the only reliable Bible. Far better a translation into Tamil or Sinhala undertaken by Sri Lankan scholars working in Sri Lanka on the basis of the Hebrew, Aramaic, and Greek originals. Sri Lankan Christians, like Christians throughout the southern hemisphere, "are constantly at the receiving end of 'packaged' gospels, discipleship courses, leadership seminars, church-growth 'gurus', even sermons and 'worship' DVDs from rich churches abroad. The latter have no desire to learn from others and, ironically, have little impact in their own societies."[10] In this regard, Western Christians resemble the Judaizers, who also went into foreign territory with the answer that the church in Turkey and beyond "needed" without ever stopping to ask the converts what resources they felt they needed in order to grow more in discipleship and extend their own mission in their own region.

But the onus was on the Galatians, not on Paul and not even on the rival teachers, to discern what was contextually appropriate and what was in keeping with their experience of God through the Spirit of God's Son. Paul blames them for not exercising their responsibility and not sufficiently trusting their experience and discernment of the Spirit. And so, perhaps, Paul would also place the responsibility on Sri Lankan Christians to find the confidence that comes from recognizing and learning to follow God's Spirit and thus not to be tossed to and fro by every strange wind that blows in from the West or from other quarters.

Following Western church paradigms, many churches in Sri Lanka have become program-focused and program-driven, putting a lot of energy into having strong and winsome activities for youth, Sunday school, children, outreach, and the like, but in the end inviting the congregation and community to see themselves as consumers rather than producers and taking energy and focus away from the relational base required to apply, for example, the kind of restorative discipline prescribed by Paul (Gal 6:1). Sri Lankan Christians listen to Western Christian voices emphasizing the importance of seeker sensitivity, buying at the same

---

[10]http://vinothramachandra.wordpress.com/2010/10/01/authentic-partnerships/ (accessed June 14, 2011).

time into the market mentality that infuses much Western material on evangelism and church growth.

It is a fine thing to learn about church growth strategies that seem to be working in the West, but before adopting and imitating those practices Sri Lankan Christians need to ask some contextual questions. Whether or not North Americans should be building megachurches, is the model of the megachurch right for Sri Lankan Christianity? Or, is the progress of the gospel and of growth in discipleship better served by many smaller congregations working together but providing the person-centered and relationship-centered matrix that is so vital a part of Sri Lankan culture? Is church growth an appropriate goal in the Sri Lankan context, or is the multiplication of a network of small churches more appropriate? Or, should a focus more explicitly on Christian growth in terms of growth in discipleship and service be at the center in Sri Lankan churches, and let the numbers go where they will?

Can Christ be worshiped in a Sri Lankan manner? What expressions would Sri Lankan Christian poets and composers give to their faith, and how would this elevate facets of Christian experience, hope, understanding, and mission of far greater relevance and importance in the context of Christian worship? It is fine to select hymns and songs composed by Western sisters and brothers for use in worship in Sri Lankan churches, but not at the expense of Sri Lankan hymnists and songwriters finding their own voice and adding their "new song" to the praise of God and the Lamb.

Christian Witness and Outreach in a Hostile Environment

Sri Lankan Christians can far more readily relate to the dynamics of persecution to which Paul alludes throughout Galatians than can readers in the United States. They occasionally encounter people who are zealous watchdogs for the Sinhalese Buddhist traditions, much as Paul had been a zealous watchdog for the Jewish covenant, and much as similar watchdogs for the Jewish covenant appear to stand behind the impetus on the part of some Jewish Christian teachers to bring the whole Christian movement closer in line with observance of the Mosaic law. During the past two years, Sri Lankan Christians (from Roman Catholic to Assemblies of God) have experienced persecution in a number of ways. A group of fifty Buddhist monks led protests against, and posted threatening placards at, a place of Christian worship; various acts of arson and vandalism were committed against places of Christian worship and the homes of Christian ministers and laity; some Christian clergy met with violent, physical assault.[11]

When we spoke together, then, about the motivations that Paul alleged to drive the rival teachers (Gal 6:12–13), there was a great deal of sympathy in the room for those rival teachers. Paul's stance in regard to embracing hostility where fidelity to the call of God necessitated the same (5:11; 6:17) posed a poignant challenge to these students and ministers.

Some of these watchdogs for the more ancient religion are well placed in politics or appear among powerful lobbying groups near to those in power, leading to serious consideration of an anti-conversion bill ("Prohibition of Forced Conversion" Bill) and to allegations of "unethical conversion" where relief work among the poor is connected with preaching a conversionist message. Such allegations are attributable in part to the legacy of colonialism. During the various periods of colonization, better jobs within the colonial administration and its support systems would often be offered to the extent that people converted to the religion of the colonizers, and aid might be restricted only to those who converted to that particular denomination from which aid was being sought.

This came to bear in our discussions about "remembering the poor" (Gal 2:10), which is a pressing need in Sri Lanka and an important venue for Christian witness. As the proposed bill represents the crystallization of a fair sector of public opinion, many Sri Lankan churches are tempted to focus their efforts more on relief without evangelizing in order to become more acceptable and provoke less hostility from the more powerful majority that feels threatened when individuals turn from the ancestral religions to the Christian faith. Others have become more cautious about engaging in relief work, focusing instead on preaching the gospel only, leaving social work to charitable organizations and the social services department. While churches as well as individual disciples are rightly cautioned not to attach conditions to charitable aid, God calls disciples both to witness to what they have found in Christ and to extend charitable aid, compelled by Christ's own love.

---

[11] Such reports are conveniently collected at http://www.persecution.org/category/countries/asia/sri-lanka/, and the details of many are familiar from stories that some of my students related firsthand.

Paul pointed to his suffering for Christ as proof of his genuineness (Gal 6:17). The marks on his body were a testimony to his faithfulness to his commission and his Commissioner, communicating that he was faithful to preach and practice the truth of the gospel when it would have been far easier and more comfortable to alter it here and there so as to avoid opposition and hostility. My conversation partners could resonate deeply and personally with this. The "marks of Christ" or "marks of a Christian" are not the wearing of a cross on a chain or the donning of a WWJD ("What would Jesus do?") bracelet or carrying the Bible everywhere. The "marks" involve developing Christ-like character and cultivating the fruit of the Spirit (Gal 5:22–23), showing Jesus himself branded in their lives so that, in any situation, they must be only what Jesus would have them be, even if that resulted in marks on their feelings and bodies, as others express their rage and prejudice against Christianity through violence.

Conclusion

How does this make a difference in the way we might read Galatians (or Scripture) in our churches and classrooms? How does this make a difference in the way we might conceive of doing ministry?

Facets of Galatians that we might pass over remain the stimulus, among Sri Lankan Christians, for lively conversation and exploration of their own context. I have never before wrestled with the implications of Gal 3:23–4:11 for people coming to Christ from a Buddhist or Hindu or Muslim background, for example, but this is a truly pressing question for the growing limbs of the body of Christ. Doing global theology, including theology of missions, must include addressing such questions in conversation with our sisters and brothers abroad.

While we may balk at considering how we have historically resembled the Judaizers, at least in terms of seeking to replicate our practices and ethos among Christians in foreign cultures, we need to become even more discerning in terms of how our involvement in a particular country, for example, Sri Lanka, nurtures the growth of Sri Lankan Christianity and how it nurtures the Westernization of Sri Lankan Christianity (often in concert with the Westernization of Sri Lanka occurring through other venues). Jesus wants to take on Sri Lankan flesh, coming to life there as he did both in Judea and in Galatia in very different ways, and Sri Lankan churches need to worship, function, and grow in Sri Lankan ways—in part, so as to have a positive effect and witness there.

Some of those indigenous ways, moreover, are better suited to bringing to life the kind of vision Paul was nurturing for Christian community than the Western ways that are supplanting the same. Sri Lankans are historically more people-focused than program-focused, more rooted in community and community-based identity than individualism and high boundaries between "private/personal" and "public." They are culturally more apt to living out Gal 5:13–6:10, I think, than we are in the West—so the more we make them like us in those ways, the more we place stumbling blocks in the path of their discipleship.

Replicating *our* denominational fragmentation in countries where Christianity will be a minority faith, and often a quite unempowered segment of the population, does the church in those countries no favors, and we should rethink how we conduct missions abroad. Who knows: it might even lead to less fragmentation here.

The intentionality on the part of at least a sizeable proportion of Sri Lankan Christians to shape church life in a way that fosters racial reconciliation in Christ, and their understanding of the power of this witness in their context, challenges us in our Christian practice of largely separate tables. They even challenge us to worship together across linguistic barriers for the sake of celebrating the greater unity and diversity of the people of God.

Western Christians come across as saying, in effect, "God has shown us that this works for us, and it will work for you as well, so here's how to do it." This attitude is reflected in our ability to market prepackaged programs and strategies to Sri Lankan churches. We may not be trying to make them after our image, though I suspect we would be most comfortable with them if we did (like the Judaizers), but we are certainly facilitating their making themselves after our image, perhaps insofar as we are not sufficiently sensitive to the impact of colonization and ongoing globalization of the West on the mindset of the colonized and the developing nations.[12]

For Further Reading

deSilva, David A. *Global Readings: A Sri Lankan Commentary on Paul's Letter to the Galatians.* Eugene, OR: Cascade, 2011.

---

[12] The author wishes to thank the trustees and administrators of the Lilly Theological Research Grants Program, which made this research possible through the award of a Faculty Fellowship for the 2010–2011 year.

Fernando, Ajith. Acts. *The NIV Application Commentary*. Grand Rapids, MI, 1998.

Holt, John Clifford, ed. *The Sri Lanka Reader: History, Culture, Politics*. Durham, NC: Duke University Press, 2011.

Ramachandra, Vinoth. *Subverting Global Myths: Theology and the Public Issues Shaping Our World*. Downers Grove, IL: InterVarsity Press, 2008.

Sugirtharajah, R. S. *Postcolonial Criticism and Biblical Interpretation*. Oxford: Oxford University Press, 2002.

Chapter 4

Response: What Does Sri Lanka Have to Do with Galatia? The Hermeneutical Challenges, Benefits, and Potential of Global Readings of Scripture

Nijay Gupta

Introduction

I wish to thank David deSilva for sharing the hermeneutical and pastoral insights from his experience in Sri Lanka so cogently and succinctly. For too many years, the voices of wise interpreters of Scripture and skilled reading communities have been neglected in view of a kind of hermeneutical hegemony of Western scholarship. I have been pleased, in more recent days, to see this beginning to change. Just in the last handful of years I have read several books attempting to open biblical and theological conversations up to a worldwide community. In 2009 and 2010, I was delighted to see the Africa Bible Commentary series (Zondervan) in print with volumes on Galatians and the Pastoral Epistles. Also, the recent *Blackwell Companion to Paul* includes a chapter on "African Readings of Paul" by Grant LeMarquand.[1] Finally, the reference work entitled *Dictionary for Theological Interpretation of the Bible* includes entries pertaining to interpretive distinctives and tendencies from Latin America, Asia, Africa, and elsewhere.[2]

---

[1] Grant LeMarquand, "African Readings of Paul," in *Blackwell Companion to Paul* (ed. S. Westerholm; Wiley-Blackwell Companions to Religion; Chichester: Wiley-Blackwell, 2011), 488–503.

[2] Kevin J. Vanhoozer, ed., *Dictionary for Theological Interpretation of the Bible* (Grand Rapids: Baker Academic, 2005).

The question I wish to pursue in my response to deSilva is this: *What is the hermeneutical gain of pursuing a global, and particularly a Sri Lankan, reading of Galatians?* If Tertullian, in his time, was compelled to ask, "What does Athens have to do with Jerusalem?" I wonder, "What does Sri Lanka have to do with Galatia?" How does being in Sri Lanka—living in that space and culture with its unique heritage and worldview—contribute to the reading and interpreting of Scripture? From reading deSilva's compelling statements in "Neither Tamil Nor Sinhalese: Reading Galatians with Sri Lankan Christians" (ch. 3), it is clear there are benefits, but I am also interested in the possible pitfalls, and I wonder about how we can bring such readings to their fullest potential. Will different *types* of readings or different *purposes* of readings more readily benefit from global perspectives? Are some global perspectives more beneficial than others? While we can dig only rather briefly and all too superficially into these dense questions, it is my intention to offer responsive reflections along these lines to deSilva's stimulating contribution.

Searching for Meaning through Triangulation

Until rather recently in history, biblical scholars dwelt on "the world *of* the text" (the meaning of the canonical text as a literary unit) and "the world *behind* the text" (the sociohistorical and literary processes and factors that brought the canonical text into being). However, now we have wisely come to acknowledge there is a world *in front of the text*—the history of readers and communities that have preserved, translated, and interpreted the text throughout history. It is naïve to think we can do exegetical analysis that gets back to the original meaning, all the while ignoring the history of how the text has been read by our predecessors.

While few would argue against taking seriously the world in front of the text as an important third context of biblical interpretation, it has pressed the question of meaning—to quote Kevin Vanhoozer's well-known book title on this subject, *Is There Meaning in the Text?* By focusing attention on the *readers* of the biblical text, questions have been raised about *their* role not only in *finding* meaning but also perhaps as actors in the process of *creating* meaning. While I find it valuable to be cognizant of the experiences, presuppositions, interests, and worldview of readers and communities as exegesis is performed, I have always been wary of giving readers the weight of *producing* meaning.

I am particularly appreciative, then, of deSilva's language of triangulation, which emphasizes both the subjective and objective aspects of meaning. Sometimes I fear that a reader-focused hermeneutic ends up being a "here is what I get out of the text" kind of approach, which can go in some troubling directions. Triangulation means that there is a real, objective meaning, but we can hardly determine it from one position alone. The more pings, the more opportunity to zero in on the location, or perhaps more realistically to eliminate places where it is *not*.[3] This underscores the deep need for a community of interpretation. Self-discovery is important, but communal dialogue in interpretation is essential.

Culturally Determined Meaning

I also appreciated the points deSilva made regarding the oft-necessary reminder that, for North Americans, biblical interpretation requires crossing not just time and space but culture as well. Currently, I am reading Ken Bailey's *Paul through Mediterranean Eyes: Cultural Studies in 1 Corinthians*,[4] which reminds us that we have much to learn from Arabic translations of Paul, and not just Latin, Greek, and English ones, because culture has a way of creeping into language. As Bailey's literary legacy attests, the Mediterranean culture, even today, offers a window into the world of the Bible that is so alien to people in places like North America or Western Europe.

In Asia, we see instances where cultural similarities with the biblical world have opened up opportunities to glean insights into the text. For example, Dhyanchand Carr points out how the Sermon on the Mount helped Indian Dalits to establish a "Dalit theology" based

---

[3] Christopher J. H. Wright articulates this well: "Even when we affirm (as I certainly do) that the historical and salvation-historical context of biblical texts and their authors is of primary and objective importance in discerning their meaning and their significance, the plurality of perspectives from which readers read them is also a vital factor in the hermeneutical richness of the global church. What persons of one culture bring from that culture to their reading of a text may illuminate dimensions or implications of the text itself that persons of another culture may have not seen so clearly." See *The Mission of God: Unlocking the Bible's Grand Narrative* (Downers Grove, IL: InterVarsity Press, 2006), 38.

[4] Ken Bailey, *Paul through Mediterranean Eyes: Cultural Studies in 1 Corinthians* (Downers Grove, IL: InterVarsity Press, 2011).

on a similar sociocultural context.[5] For the Dalits, bridges were built between the world of Jesus and the social context of this marginalized group in modern India in such a way as to bring the message of the canonical text alive.

Illuminated Textual Aspects

By paying attention to global readings of Scripture, it has become clear enough that various communities will inevitably find some situations and lessons from the text more relevant and applicable than others. For example, in North America it is hardly a common problem for believers to wonder whether they can eat food sacrificed to an idol. In India, though, this is a more common phenomenon. Thus, by entering a global conversation on the meaning of Scripture, we may learn from a variety of cultural readers who can illuminate certain textual aspects based on their analogous experiences or contexts.

In particular, deSilva makes the point that Sri Lankans can reflect and build bridges from their former religious experiences and commitments and the dominant ones of the culture, rather than seeing the relationship between past religion and present in terms of a complete (and even sometimes hostile) dismissal and abandonment. He gives the example of bringing the Christian gospel in conversation with the Dhamma. Likewise, Indian Vengal Chakkarai compared Jesus' incarnation in the Gospel of John with the Hindu concept of *avatar*, the bodily manifestation of a divine being on earth.[6] This, of course, is not too different from what the apostle Paul did when he quoted the Greek poets Epimenides and Menander.

North American Christians, like myself, do not tend to think through how to enter into dialogue about Christianity with other religions, largely because we experience the freedom of being the dominant faith group among our people. In fact, my guess would be that, for many Christians in my context, interfaith dialogue is viewed as a practice that inevitably weakens personal faith. However, in places like India and Sri

---

[5] See D. Carr, "A Biblical Basis for Dalit Theology," in *Indigenous People: Dalits: Dalit Issues in Today's Theological Debate* (ed. J. Massey; Delhi: SPCK, 1994), 231–49.

[6] See A. A. Yewangoe, *Theologia Crucis in Asia: Asian Christian Views on Suffering in the Face of Overwhelming Poverty and Multifaceted Religiosity in Asia* (Amsterdam: Rodopi, 1987), 59.

Lanka, it is necessary for survival and growth (as it was for early Christianity for some time)!

Applying Scripture in Various Contexts

As one reads deSilva's contribution, he moves somewhat seamlessly from Sri Lankan *readings* or *interpretations* of the biblical text to Sri Lankan *applications* of the text. No doubt the students and wider community he was in dialogue with during his time there did not even know they were moving to and from these steps.

DeSilva observes how Gal 3:26–29, with its disorienting and destabilizing statement about new creation and social values, struck a resounding chord for the Sri Lankan believers. By being attentive to global readings of Scripture, we can see the complexity of how it is applied in various contexts.

I spent some time, about a decade ago, in the former Yugoslavia Republic of Macedonia, and it was a distinct pleasure to see Christian Macedonians and Christian Albanians, who ethnically are often in violent conflict in the culture at large, sit side by side and worship and pray together to the same God. Few would question the ways in which this kind of unity and reconciliation was restorative and refreshing.

DeSilva also raises the matter of family, and how Scripture, religion, and culture contribute in unique ways to how such relationships work. For example, as he brings up the role of the father or husband in the family in Sri Lanka, my wife and I have had to think through the Indian tradition of touching the feet of elders as a sign of respect. We have always done this when visiting Hindu family and friends in India, and no one has questioned or doubted our Christian faith. However, when we did this in front of some of our Indians friends who were *Christians*, they were deeply offended and told us, "Christians do not participate in the touching of the feet tradition, as it is a form of idolatry." This is part of the age-old Christ-and-culture debate. When do we take a stand against cultural expressions we find offensive and when do we integrate? Do we integrate and explain how our thinking is different? Do we separate and explain why it is a make-or-break issue? Do we integrate and yet seek to change the cultural expression? Do we separate and yet seek to change it? Does Scripture call all people in all places to take one kind of stance, or is application *contextualized*? If it is contextualized, to what degree?

Challenged by Global Readings

Part of the significance of listening to global readings of Scripture is to learn from the perspective of other people in other cultures and spaces. Sometimes we need to hear their voices and see the things they notice that we do not. Sometimes we need to understand their processes of interpretation. Sometimes, though, we need to be corrected by them in ways big and small.

In particular, deSilva notes that the Sri Lankan Christians took interest in the matter of the *stoicheia* in Galatians. While this term came up in the study of Galatians, I have been examining it in my current research on Colossians.[7] Just as there is a cultural interest in horoscopes and astrology in Sri Lanka, so it is in India—I recall that in my childhood my mother tried to read my palm! Paying attention to the influence of spiritual forces, something we in North America feel quite enlightened enough to belittle and dismiss as superstition, is, in fact, a part of everyday life in places like Sri Lanka, India, and Africa. Edwin Ahirika argues that Africa has a continental-cultural worldview, where there are witches and wizards who hunt and harness people and that they owe their occult powers to the *nyama* or psychic energy of the earth.[8] There are invisible ghosts and spirits with great power that can be manipulated. Ahirika notes that Western Christians have come and told them they are fools to believe in spirits or ghosts, but Ahirika urges that there is no good reason to discount the African worldview, especially in view of the relevance of the discussion of spiritual powers by Paul in texts like Ephesians, Galatians, and Colossians. Perhaps we have something to learn from *their* perspective and experience.[9] Respected North American New Testament scholar Craig Keener has had the humility and attentive heart to raise

---

[7] The point that many faith communities (especially in Asia and Africa) in the global church carry a strong belief in spiritual forces, miraculous healing, and the existence of evil is underscored by Timothy C. Tennent in *Theology in the Context of World Christianity: How the Global Church Is Influencing the Way We Think about and Discuss Theology* (Grand Rapids: Zondervan, 2007).

[8] See E. A. Ahirika, "Contextualization of Ephesians 6:12: Liberation of African Christians from the Fear of Principalities," *Sevartham* 25 (2000): 59–76.

[9] Philip Jenkins tells the story of a meeting between some North American Episcopalians and African Anglicans who debated about the issue of homosexuality and its scriptural legitimacy. The African bishop became incensed when he came under the impression that the Episcopalians were not taking the Scriptures seriously, and he blurted, "If you don't *believe* the Scripture, why did

these questions regarding the phenomonological aspects of healing and miraculous works that get reported around the world but are so quickly denied in places like North America and Europe. In *Miracles*,[10] he wonders whether we Western scholars have been trapped inside of Hume's limited worldview for too long and have epistemologically muffled the voices of people all around the world that testify to the miraculous work of God.

Conclusion

One important lesson we learn about Scripture from these kinds of conversations is its inexhaustible richness. Each biblical text may not always be relevant, in every part, all of the time, to every person, but we are unwise to believe we have mastered it or tapped out its kerygmatic and prophetic energy. Whether Tamil or Sinhalese, Macedonian or Albanian, in Seattle or in Boston, we thank God for all the members of the body of Christ that bring wholeness. In response to the wise words of David deSilva, I say "Jai"—which in Hindi means "Amen!"

For Further Reading

deSilva, David A. *Global Readings: A Sri Lankan Commentary on Paul's Letter to the Galatians*. Eugene, OR: Cascade, 2011.

Flemming, Dean. *Contextualization in the New Testament: Patterns for Theology and Mission*. Downers Grove, IL: InterVarsity Press, 2005.

Kitzberger, Ingrid Rosa, ed. *The Personal Voice in Biblical Interpretation*. London: Routledge, 1999.

Liew, Tat-siong Benny. "Asian Criticism." Pages 184–91 in *Searching for Meaning*. Edited by P. Gooder. Louisville: Westminster John Knox, 2008.

Tennent, Timothy C. *Theology in the Context of World Christianity: How the Global Church Is Influencing the Way We Think about and Discuss Theology*. Grand Rapids: Zondervan, 2007.

---

you bring it to us in the first place?" (*The New Faces of Christianity: Believing the Bible in the Global South* [Oxford: Oxford University Press, 2006], 1).

[10] Craig S. Keener, *Miracles: The Credibility of the New Testament Accounts* (2 vols.; Grand Rapids: Baker Academic, 2011).

Chapter 5

Word Becoming Flesh
[On Appropriation]:
Engaging Daniel as a Survival Manual

Barbara M. Leung Lai

Appropriation is a two-way trip from the world of the Danielic text to the contextual situatedness of the reader (or vice versa). To begin any discussion on appropriation with a reflection on self-identity on the part of the reader is, therefore, a significant point of departure.

Who Am I?

Asking "Who am I?" signifies a self-reflective process rather than an assumed identity statement of "who I am." If the same question were asked two decades ago, I would have formulated my answer in the realm of race and ethnicity, gender, culture, and the social location of reading.[1] Addressing this question today entails also a consideration of context, situatedness, as well as one's lived experience. This essay seeks to provide a demonstrated example of perspectival reading as well as its appropriation (i.e., Daniel as a survival manual). My self-identity will naturally have some bearing on my representation.

I begin with a commonly accepted maxim: the postmodern self is socially constructed, fluidic, and multiple.[2] Randy Litchfield has stated

---

[1] Fernando F. Segovia and Mary Ann Tolbert, eds., *Reading from This Place*, vol. 1: *Social Location and Biblical Interpretation in the United States*; vol. 2: *Social Location and Biblical Interpretation in Global Perspective* (Minneapolis: Fortress, 1995).

[2] Randy G. Litchfield, "Rethinking Local Bible Study in a Postmodern Era," in *Paradigms for Bible Study: The Bible in the Third Millennium* (ed. Robert Fowler et al.; New York: T&T Clark, 2004), 236. In fact, postmodern theorists

that self "is not centered in one location, but decentered across many social settings. . . . We are many selves that must be orchestrated into coherence, an ongoing process that we recognize as our identity."[3]

Since self is a complex, elusive concept, therefore self-engagement in constructing one's self-identity is pivotal. I intend to approach my self-identity here from a new angle of perception, namely, the "external shaping forces" that continuously mold me into who I am as a shepherd-teacher (Eph 4:11) and scholar-saint (in the words of John Stott). Yet collapsing my specific ethnic-sociocultural identity as Chinese-Canadian in the academy[4] would potentially or reversely[5] silence my voice and diminish my influence (should there be any) on contextual biblical interpretation and perspectival reading of the chosen text—which is, to a certain extent, I suppose, the anticipated outcome of this essay.

External Shaping Forces

Theologically trained both in the East and West, I had the privilege of acquiring the best of both worlds. Teaching cross-culturally in Canada and the United States, South and Central America, Ukraine, Hong Kong, Southeast Asia, and China has collectively shaped my teaching career. This experience has imparted to me a moderate degree of competency in adapting to culturally diverse learning communities. With my allegiance to the interpretive community where evangelical biblical scholarship is nurtured and promoted among practitioners of postmodern interpretive methods, I have been immensely affected by my predecessors and colleagues.[6]

---

differ considerably about the determinacy of the context and the agency of the self (cf. 236–37).

[3] Ibid., 236–37.

[4] A collection of essays on "Reading in Between: Biblical Interpretation in Canada" is being considered for publication in Brill's *Biblical Interpretation* series. As a Chinese-Canadian woman scholar, I have contributed a chapter to this volume.

[5] In the past two decades, in terms of the effect of the collective Asian interpretive voice, I witness the shift from a marginalized status to gaining a moderate degree of prominence in the academy. Yet, if any race- or culture-specific voice fails to affirm its culturally shaped and contextual distinctiveness, it would potentially be minimized or reduced to voiceless again.

[6] To name a few, John E. Goldingay's narrative approach to constructing OT theology (*Old Testament Theology* [3 vols.], vol. 1: *Israel's Gospel*; vol. 2:

My six-year appointment as one of the pioneering members of the Committee on Race and Ethnicity (CORE) at the Association of Theological School (ATS) has provided many cross-feeding forums for culture-specific and cross-cultural dialogues among African-American, Hispanic, Asian-American, and First Nation faculty members and administrators. My service in the past two years as a member of the Advisory Council of "Women in Leadership in Theological Education" (WiL) at ATS has tremendously shaped my perspectives on gender issues in theological leadership. Most significant of all, teaching for fifteen years at my current institution, known as one of the most culturally diverse student communities in North America, has immensely enriched me in fulfilling my role as a shepherd-teacher.

As a prime-timer engaging in the flesh-and-blood collective lived experience of my faith community—a mega, multicultural, and multigenerational ethnic church in metro Toronto—has further enabled me to have the capacity to read the Danielic text contextually: Despite present chaotic situations, God is still in control.

These are my life contexts (or in the words of Thiselton, "life-worlds"[7]), and the result of this more or less narrative approach to my self-identity indicates, on the one hand, that my self is still unfinalized. Yet, on the other hand, there are layers of lived contextual experience that are being accumulated into my ever enriching and dynamic self. One cannot seek to construct the message of Daniel in a vacuum or within the borders of a loosely defined framework of Chinese-Canadian or Asian-American

---

Israel's Faith; vol. 3: *Israel's Life* [Downers Grove, IL: IVP Academic, 2003, 2006, 2009]); Anthony C. Thiselton's elaboration on the "capacity to transform" for texts and readers, and providing a conceptual framework for the "hermeneutics of self-involvement" (see *New Horizons in Hermeneutics,* chaps. 1, 8 [London: HarperCollins, 1992]); the refreshing perspectives and approaches to biblical interpretation provided by Craig G. Bartholomew (e.g., in *After Pentecost: Language and Biblical Interpretation* [ed. Craig G. Bartholomew et al.; Grand Rapids: Zondervan, 2001]; and *Ecclesiastes* [BCOTWP; Grand Rapids: Baker Academic, 2008]).

[7] Thistleton, *New Horizons,* 247–52. David R. Blumenthal draws on the same concept and refers to the whole flesh-and-blood life experience of an individual as a "text-of-life" (see *Facing the Abusing God: A Theology of Protest* [Louisville: Westminster John Knox, 1993], esp. 61). Cf. my employment of the concept in developing a theology of lament and protest contextually in Barbara M. Leung Lai, "Psalm 44 and the Function of Lament and Protest," *OTE* 20, no. 2 (2007): 418–31.

reading. As I put my world in front of the world of the text, I have to approach the text self-engagingly out of my different life contexts.

Tools and Parameters

In this reading of Daniel, I operate with a text-anchored and reader-oriented model in biblical interpretation. I seek to incorporate the three worlds of the text (the world behind, the world of, and the world in front of the text).[8] In essence, any three-world approach to the biblical text would necessitate an integration of competing methods and tools. Engaging the apocalyptic text of Daniel with this holistic approach entails a reading strategy that seeks to integrate several sets of polarities: diachronic and synchronic; objective and pragmatic (subjective); and historical-critical and empirical (or experiential). My point of departure is to approach the task with a view that the three worlds are intimately interconnected and that the interface of text and reader shapes all three worlds.

As a demonstrated example, my reading exemplifies an intentional effort to move from meaning to the two dimensions of contemporary significance: what it means to the Christian church at large and what it means to me as individual member of the faith community contextually. The three procedural steps together should be considered as a complete hermeneutical cycle—from meaning to significance, or from interpretation to appropriation. This interpretive process should be considered as the ultimate goal of *any* interpretive task.[9]

Four components that make up competency in biblical interpretation are at work here: mind, will, emotion, and imagination. The demand for a sound analytical mind (e.g., to identify the multiplicity of speaking voices and the significant sets of repetitions in the narrative description of Dan 3); the will in living out the hope and trust as embedded in the

---

[8] Cf. Randolph W. Tate, *Biblical Interpretation: An Integrated Approach* (3d ed.; Peabody, MA: Hendrickson, 2008).

[9] The SBL promotion (2011 annual meeting) of the featured session on "Romans through History and Culture" states that the group "respects diverging interpretations by acknowledging that any interpretation of a text of Scripture necessarily involves three interpretive choices: an analytical choice, a hermeneutical/theological choice, and a contextual choice" (SBL president's letter, November 1, 2011). I would like to restate that these are not to be perceived as three alternative interpretive agendas undertaken by the interpreter but three pivotal steps to complete an interpretive cycle for any given text.

overarching message of the book ("in spite of the present appearances, God is in control"[10]); engaging our emotions in taking Daniel on his own terms and immersing ourselves in the visionary experience as he describes it;[11] and the capacity to exercise our imagination in character profiling (e.g., comparing the two characters, King Darius and Daniel in Dan 6).

Reading: Engaging Daniel as a Survival Manual[12]

I concur with Mark G. Brett that, as a methodological procedure, any talk about reading strategy must be preceded by an analysis of interpretive interest; a reading strategy "will only be coherent if it is guided by a clearly articulated question or goal."[13] Following this schema, my reading strategy of Daniel is goal-oriented and tailor-made to suit the objective of this essay—a version of perspectival reading (i.e., reading Daniel as a survival manual) and its appropriation to both immigrant families or minorities in the profession and to the community of pastors. This is also representative of my core interpretive interest—the characterization of Daniel in its two dimensions: the public Daniel (Dan 1–6) and the private Daniel (Dan 7–12). I have adopted John Goldingay's recommended approach in reading Daniel here; to him, "the best approach is to take him on his own terms and immerse ourselves in the visionary experience as he describes it."[14]

---

[10] This is also the identified core message in Tremper Longman III, *Daniel* (NIVAC; Grand Rapids: Zondervan, 1999), 13.

[11] John E. Goldingay, *Daniel* (WBC 30; Dallas: Word, 1987), xl.

[12] For a more comprehensive methodological orientation and exegetical basis of this reading, please refer to Barbara Leung Lai, *Through the "I"-Window: The Inner Life of Characters in the Old Testament* (HBM 34; Sheffield: Sheffield Phoenix Press, 2011), chaps. 2–3; "Daniel," in *The People's Bible* (Philadelphia: Fortress, 2009), 1014–15; "Aspirant Sage or Dysfunctional Seer? Cognitive Dissonance and Pastoral Vulnerability in the Profile of Daniel," *PastPsych* 57, nos. 3–4 (2008): 199–210.

[13] Mark G. Brett, "Four or Five Things to Do with Texts: A Taxonomy of Interpretive Interests," in *The Bible in Three Dimensions: Essays in Celebration of Forty Years of Biblical Studies in the University of Sheffield* (ed. D. J. A. Clines et al.; Sheffield: JSOT Press, 1990), 357 (357–77).

[14] Goldingay, *Daniel*, xl, cites S. Niditch, "The Visionary," in *Ideal Figures in Ancient Judaism* (ed. G. W. E. Nickelsburg and J. J. Collins; Chico, CA: Scholars Press, 1980), 153–79.

Point of Departure: Two Dimensions of the Danielic Self
(the Public Daniel and the Private Daniel)

In *Circle of Sovereignty,* Danna Nolan Fewell has provided the most comprehensive narrative reading of the court tales of the book (Dan 1–6). While the public Daniel emerges naturally as a figure in Fewell's literary analysis, the sage is presented as one among the other prominent characters (his three friends and the foreign kings) in the narrative framework of the book. The interiority (or being) of Daniel that could be uncovered through his "I" voice (places where the character speaks in the first person) in the apocalyptic portion of the book (Dan 7–12) is absent in Fewell's discussion. Since Fewell's seminal contribution, literary approaches to the apocalyptic portion of the book (Dan 7–12) have flourished,[15] and each in its own way has provided new angles of perception toward the overall structure of the book. However, the Danielic internal profile has never been given any attention thus far in the field of OT character studies.[16]

No Danielic characterization will be complete without attending to both the public Daniel as portrayed in the court tales of Dan 1–6 as well as the private Daniel as self-presented in the exotic visions of Dan 7–12 through his "I" voice. Failing to identity the importance of this "I"-window is, at the same time, missing an important interpretive link. In other words, this Danielic self-referential "I" in Dan 7–12 serves as a port of entry to the inner life of Daniel.

Survival in Diaspora in Service to Four Foreign Kings:
The Public Daniel

Daniel's public self as portrayed in Dan 1–6 is the epitome of self-confidence—an aspiring sage. He climbs the corporate ladder from a

---

[15] The representative examples are John E. Goldingay, "Story, Vision, Interpretation: Literary Approaches to Daniel," in *The Book of Daniel in Light of New Findings* (ed. A. S. Van der Woude; BETL 106; Leuven: Leuven University Press, 1993), 295–313; M. A. Knibb, "You Are Indeed Wiser Than Daniel: Reflections on the Character of the Book of Daniel," in ibid., 339–411; Paul L. Redditt, "Daniel 9: Its Structure and Meaning," *CBQ* 62, no. 2 (2000): 236–49; Paul J. Tanner, "The Literary Structure of the Book of Daniel," *BSac* 160, no. 3 (2003): 269–82; B. L. Woodward Jr., "Literary Strategies and Authorship in the Book of Daniel," *JETS* 37, no. 1 (1994): 39–53.

[16] In Fewell's comprehensive treatment on the characterization of Daniel, only a chapter (chap. 7) is devoted to Dan 7–12. See Fewell, *Circle of Sovereignty.*

captive prisoner to the prime minister of the whole kingdom (2:28). The summary appraisal in 6:29 [28] best captures the accomplishment of the public Daniel: "So this Daniel is made prosperous in the reign of Darius, and in the reign of Cyrus, the Persian." Time and again, the figure of a man with the spirit of the holy gods and possessing superior qualities (loosing knots, interpreting dreams and riddles) stands out distinctively among his peers.

Reading Dan 1–6 as resistance literature and as a manual for survival, the coping strategy that Daniel has adopted is a key point of entry. Two prominent readings provide two different dimensions to the coping strategy as exhibited in the characterization of the public Daniel. To Fewell, Daniel's prosperity is the result of Darius's legislation (6:29 [28]). By living his life in prosperity, Daniel is able to remain faithful to both the earthly sovereigns (Darius and Cyrus) and the Hebrew God.[17] Therefore, remaining in prosperity and in a position of power while navigating the troubled political waters requires certain wisdom, and indications of this wisdom are penetrated through the court tales in the first six chapters.[18]

The second reading is presented by David Valeta.[19] He based his work on the Russian theorist Mikhael Bakhtin's genre description of pre-novelistic Menippean satire as a conceptual framework and identification tool. Valeta reads the court tales as examples of Menippean satire and resistance literature against hegemonic regimes and control.[20] His analysis of this genre provides thought-provoking stimulations for our inquiry here. Daniel could be read as a manual for survival. The means of resisting kings and empires as reflected in Dan 1–6 is the creative use of satire and humor.[21]

Surviving His Inner Self: The Private Daniel

The twelve chapters of Daniel are not arranged in chronological order. The visions in Dan 7 and 8 occur during the reign of Belshazzar,

---

[17] Cf. ibid., 118.

[18] E.g., Daniel's request to the king for the appointment of his three friends as administrators over the province of Babylon at the opportune moment (2:48–49); restating his public role and re-establishing his high-ranking status in Dan 5; his wit and courageous resistance over conspiracy in Dan 6.

[19] David Valeta, *Lions and Ovens and Visions: Satirical Reading of Daniel 1–6* (HBM 12; Sheffield: Sheffield Phoenix Press, 2008).

[20] According to Bakhtin, this Menippean satire genre has fourteen characteristics. For a precise listing, see Valeta, *Lions and Ovens and Visions,* 118.

[21] See also Leung Lai, "Daniel," 1015.

presumably before the events of Dan 5. Daniel 9 and 6 take place during the reign of Darius. The last vision (10–12) occurs during the reign of Cyrus. An arrangement of the chronology of the chapters has important bearing on the Danielic self in that his public and private selves are simultaneously revealed within the same temporal timeframe. While he functions publicly as an aspirant sage with insight, intelligence, and outstanding wisdom to interpret dreams (5:12, 14), he simultaneously admits that the vision is beyond his understanding (8:27). Deeply troubled (7:15, 28) and exhausted by his visions, he lies ill for several days. Yet he still has to get up and attend to his public functions—the king's business (8:27). In his private self, he has to keep the matter (troubled thoughts) to himself (7:28). As Fewell has observed, the setting in Dan 7 and 8 lends further irony and depth to the scenario in Dan 5.[22] Another sharp contrast prevails as we compare the two Danielic selves. In Dan 5, a bold, self-confident Daniel confronts a weak and frightened Belshazzar. Yet in his private life, his fear is described in very much the same manner as the king's (cf. 7:15, 28; 8:17, 27 with 5:6, 9–10).

A closer look at the inner conflict of the character suggests the idea of cognitive dissonance. Daniel's ability to understand visions and dreams of all kinds is a gift from God (נתן in 1:17). He distinguishes himself among the administrators and satraps by his exceptional qualities (6:3). Living through his own visionary experience as self-presented in Dan 7–12 places him at the disjunction of his expected role as an outstanding sage and his lived experienced (as dysfunctional seer). This condition of cognitive dissonance may account for the emotional upheaval and symptoms of physical illness that the private Daniel is suffering. Yet if the overarching framework in 6:29 [28] and 12:13 is intentionally structured, the disharmony between his private and public selves can be compensated by the promissory charge in 12:13: "But you, go on to the end, and you shall rest and stand in your lot at the end of the days."

Appropriation: "Word Becoming Flesh"

Appropriation is a two-way trip from the world of the text to the contextual situatedness of the reader (or vice versa).[23] As an example

---

22 Fewell, *Circle of Sovereignty*, 121.

23 Hans-Georg Gadamer (*Truth and Method* [New York: Seabury, 1975], cited in Schuyler Brown, *Text and Psyche: Experiencing Scripture Today* [New

of perspectival reading, I intend to explicate the following two lines of appropriation here—they are both text-centered and reader-oriented.

To Immigrant Families and Minorities in the Profession

Daniel is a text peopled by members of diverse cultures. Daniel's social world is unpleasant and difficult because of foreign rule. Perseverance and the ability to adapt are necessary tools for survival. If one reads Daniel as a success story, the overall stance of the narratives in Dan 1–6 is one of loyalty, optimism and, perhaps, accommodation toward the ruling power. Crossing borders between the home and the host culture, immigrant families today have to go through the same journey of alienation, adaptation, assimilation, and, for some, reorientation. As in Daniel, pleasure or pain, success or failure are among the possibilities of this border-crossing experience in the diaspora. Likewise, remaining in a borderland experience or negotiating an ever-expanding in-between space is among the options in the life of an immigrant. Daniel exemplifies an individual's breaking away from a captive status to become an aspiring sage in an adopted culture. Failing to perceive this possibility in life, we would remain perpetual captives in a free land.

Daniel is a text that is often appropriated by people who discover that it speaks to the contexts in which they find themselves. In 9:2, Daniel himself turns to a book—Jeremiah—as he seeks to understand his present situation. In doing so, he mirrors our search for meaning and significance in our contexts. If Daniel can be read as a manual for survival—and even success—under hostile and dominating empires, yet, it is intriguing to note, as advocated by Valeta, Daniel and his group's coping strategy is the creative use of satire and humor cushioned with wisdom (not direct confrontation). This may have profound implications for coping strategies on the part of minorities today, particularly for those in the academic, religious, or theological disciplines.

York: Continuum, 1998], 47) has long been an advocate of this view. He affirms the centrality of appropriation in that in order to understand the ancient text, the interpreter "must not seek to disregard himself and his particular hermeneutical situation. He must relate the text to his situation if he wants to understand at all" (*Truth and Method*, 289).

To the "Daniel" (Potentially) in Each of Us

As a profoundly pastoral book, the effect of the inner life of Daniel on the corporate dimension—"the community of pastors"—has seldom been brought to the foreground of appropriation. As I immerse myself in the Danielic visionary experience, something intriguing happens. Yes, the world of Daniel is full of conflicts, turbulence, rising and falling of kings and kingdoms in the course of human history and beyond. It is also a world of archetypal imagery embedded in dreams and visions. Yet, as I penetrate through the service level of the text and zoom in to those deeper structures, I have been powerfully drawn to the internal world of Daniel—his private self. In other words, as the text engages my unconscious feelings, I naturally bypass the turbulent external world of Daniel and touch his inner feelings through the transference of identity. My reading takes me from the Danielic public self as an aspiring sage to my public role as a theological educator and shepherd-teacher; from his private self as a suffering and dysfunctional seer to aspects of my inner life.

Daniel's interior world is a world of paradoxes. Daniel asks but cannot comprehend the answer; he wants to know but fails to understand; he sees but cannot perceive; he hears but is unable to respond. His "I" voice is heard everywhere, and it makes me pause every time it is uttered.[24] With the postmodern consciousness of the self, my previously subdued Chinese self has been brought to the foreground as I interact with the Danielic self in its two aspects, public and private. As I *relive* the Danielic conflicting emotions and appropriate them to my context as a shepherd-teacher, I face the same dilemma of my inability to function well and live up to my role expectations.

To be able to look into the inner life of Daniel and to experience his feelings is a comforting path. In a way, my reading and emotive-experiencing event is a therapeutic exercise of appropriation. This reading is a demonstrated example of *re-expression*. The Danielic emotions are complex and psychophysical. Thus walking through this path of emotive-experiencing (*reliving*) has been exhausting! Yet at the end of

---

[24] In strategic places where Daniel discloses himself and shares with his readers his psychological or physical state, the emphatic, self-referential "I, Daniel" (אנה דניאל) is used (7:15, 28; 8:27; 10:2, 7; 12:5), inviting his readers into his inner feelings (fear, bewilderment, anxiety, struggles). As Francis Landy has concluded, "If vision suggests clarity and exteriority, voice evokes the interiority of the person and an intimation beyond the horizon" ("Vision and Voice in Isaiah," *JSOT* 88 [2000], 36 [19–36]).

the journey what has been able to calm the tormented soul has the same soothing effect upon me: "But you, [Pastor Barbara], go on to the end; for you shall rest and stand in your lot at the end of the days" (Dan 12:13). It is a serene but assuring hope.

Afterword

Interrelated Questions

Toward the end of this presentation, several interrelated questions come to mind: What constitutes the global perspective(s) in my reading? To what extent can my reading serve as an example of globalized reading? Or, alternatively, what does it mean to engage texts globally?

First, reflecting on my narrative-contextual approach to my self-identity, I have to admit that I am still very much a product of the West, including my social locations of reading. However, all biblical interpretive endeavors are in essence cross-cultural and demand a fusion of the two horizons: the horizon of the ancient text and that of the contemporary reader. To be able to identify what makes my reading an ethnic-, gender-, culture-specific representation is a rather wishful thinking. Conforming to the loosely established Chinese-Canadian or Asian-American way of reading may handicap ourselves and minimize our capacity to transform the meaning-significance of the text and the act of reading. To this end, could we legitimately speak of the consequences of globalized biblical interpretation?

Second, given the fact that the audience of this essay are all trained readers, what makes it a uniquely Leung Lai reading that reflects, to a certain extent, a Chinese-Canadian woman's reading? Perhaps it is the continual external shaping forces that collectively play a strategic role in shaping my interpretive interests (the case in point is the Danielic internal profile), as well as the conscious demand for self-involvement in engaging texts out of my life contexts.

Third, perceiving globalization as both a dynamic movement and a challenge, we are reminded to embrace diversity and multiplicity of interpretive voices interdisciplinarily. We must be cautious of stereotyping.

Word Becoming Flesh: Toward an Appropriation Theory

Word Becoming Flesh: Wisdom and Appropriation is the working title of my sabbatical book project. Three conceptual terms have been referred to in this presentation, and they are interconnected: global-ization, contextualization, and appropriation. I find "appropriation" is more or less a more encompassing term. While appropriation and rel-evance theories are at the core of research across many disciplines, the goal of working out an appropriation theory has to aim at, first and foremost, its global applicability. The act of appropriation involves the engagement of one's self out of one's life contexts and situatedness.

According to Andrew Kille, "appropriation involves not only an analysis of various aspects of the text, it requires a *re-expression* of those elements in a way that the reader can grasp."[25] Schuyler Brown further articulates the vibrant dynamics of the act of appropriation. Appro-priation takes place in the imaginative space between the reader's own world and the possible world projected by the text. It is controlled nei-ther by the objectivity of the text alone nor by the subjectivity of the reader. Appropriation occurs in the lively intersection between text and reader.[26]

The following slice of my lived experience best explains the act of appropriation: that is, from *reliving* to *re-expressing*. Kazoh Kitamori was probably the first Asian theologian to have contributed to the the-ology of the pain of God. The English version of his monograph was published in the mid-1960s. In identifying himself with the pain and suffering of the Japanese nation during the aftermath of the atomic bomb, he wrote the insightful and penetrating book, *Theology of the Pain of God.*[27] As a young seminarian reading his work in the early 1970s, I was profoundly impressed by the depth of his insights and the level of his engagement in the subject. As Kitamori *relived* the na-tional suffering and shame and *re-expressed* the emotional pain through the production of his book, the same transitive impact was made on me. I hope this illustration may illuminate the act and dynamics of appropriation.

Appropriation, "Word Becoming Flesh," is both an *indicative* and an *imperative* in the task of biblical interpretation.

---

[25] D. Andrew Kille, *Psychological Biblical Criticism* (GBS/OT; Minneapolis: Augsburg Fortress, 2001), 53.

[26] Brown, *Text and Psyche*, 25.

[27] Kazoh Kitamori, *Theology of the Pain of God* (Richmond: John Knox, 1965).

For Further Reading

Fewell, Danna Nolan. *Circle of Sovereignty: A Story of Stories in Daniel 1–6.* Journal for the Study of the Old Testament: Supplement Series 72. Sheffield: Almond, 1988.

Hesselgrave, David J., and Edward Rommen. *Contextualization: Meanings, Methods, and Models.* Pasadena, CA: William Carey Library, 2003.

Knut, Holter, and Louis C. Jonker, eds. *Global Hermeneutics? Reflections and Consequences.* International Organization for the Study of the Old Testament Congress. Atlanta: Society of Biblical Literature, 2010.

Foskett, Mary F., and Jeffrey Kah-Jin Kuan, eds. *Ways of Being, Ways of Reading: Asian American Biblical Interpretation.* St. Louis: Chalice, 2006.

Leung Lai, Barbara M. "Aspirant Sage or Dysfunctional Seer? Cognitive Dissonance and Pastoral Vulnerability in the Profile of Daniel." *PastPsych* 57 (2008): 199–210.

Tate, Randolph W. *Biblical Interpretation: An Integrated Approach.* 3d ed. Peabody, MA: Hendrickson, 2008.

CHAPTER 6

Response: Reflections on Self and Survival

Chloe Sun

I would like to thank the Institute for Biblical Research for giving me the opportunity to respond to Dr. Barbara Leung Lai's presentation. I also would like to thank Dr. Lai for giving me the opportunity to read through the book of Daniel one more time.

First of all, I commend Leung Lai's insightful reading of Daniel. I can resonate with her essay with all my inner being. By taking Daniel on his own terms and immersing herself in the visionary experience of Daniel, Leung Lai's reading is one that honors the text as well as engages the reader in a personal and powerful way. As a responder, I thought, "Why not use her own method to respond?" Therefore, in the remainder of this response, I will comment on three areas from Leung Lai's essay, after immersing myself in her description of herself and her reading of Daniel. I will also add a little of my own narrative along the way.

Being and Doing

At the beginning of her essay, Leung Lai raises the question "Who am I?" This question of "Who am I?" has also been one that I constantly wrestle with. As a Chinese raised in two countries in East Asia and educated in the United States, teaching at an ethnic seminary, ministering to multigenerational immigrant churches, and now going to a white church, I too must make sense of a decentered self—a self rooted in multiple social settings. I believe it is only out of this ever-changing and multifaceted self in different contexts that a global reading is possible and credible.

Leung Lai draws attention to the external shaping forces that help to forge her understanding of self, specifically her understanding of herself as a "scholar-saint" as well as a "shepherd-teacher." I also see myself as a scholar-saint and a shepherd-teacher, perhaps due to similar external shaping forces in my context. Like Leung Lai, I am also Chinese, female, and an immigrant in North America. I am also closely associated with a faith community, teaching in the same field (OT/HB), facing similar struggles as a minority in the profession, negotiating my identity, and trying to make sense of who I am in the in-between space.

However, despite the functional identity of scholar-saint and shepherd-teacher, Leung Lai and I are distinct individuals with unique identities. I wholeheartedly agree that the roles of scholar-saint and shepherd-teacher are integral parts of who we are. I want to highlight, as well, that apart from our functional identities shaped by similar external forces are identities that hold constant, having nothing to do with our function or what we do. Rather, this part of our identity lies in our very being. This includes but is not limited to our distinct personalities, temperaments, and interests—the things in us that hold us steady regardless of our external forces.

I want to emphasize that I wholeheartedly agree with Leung Lai that external forces are important in shaping who we are. Her essay helps me revisit those external forces that shaped my own functional identity, and for that I am grateful.

The Two Dimensions of the Danielic Self

In her essay, Leung Lai distinguishes two sides of Daniel, the public and the private. The public Daniel is portrayed in Dan 1–6, describing his success story as a court official. The private Daniel is depicted in Dan 7–12 and is revealed through his first-person pronoun—"I." Leung Lai states that this "I" voice uncovers the interiority of Daniel and serves as a "port of entry" to his inner life. As I read through the book of Daniel one more time, I too cannot help but notice the frequent appearance of the "I" voice in Dan 7–12. Many times, this "I" voice is emphatic—"I, Daniel" (*ani dani'el*), which stresses its significance in communicating Daniel's inner voice and his eyewitness account of the events.

Leung Lai's differentiation of the two dimensions of the Danielic self provides a helpful lens for readers to perceive Daniel as a realistic and flesh-and-blood human being. I agree with Leung Lai's general thrust on this insight, yet I would like to raise a friendly question on whether this public-private dichotomy is portrayed in such a strict clear-cut manner in the text. Do the public and private Daniel coalesce and overlap at times? Are there traces of the inner life of Daniel portrayed in Dan 1–6?

When I contemplate the two dimensions of Daniel, the role of prayer comes to mind. In Dan 2:20–23, when the mystery of King Nebuchadnezzar's dream was made known to Daniel in a night vision, Daniel prayed to God and said, "I acknowledge and praise you, O God of my fathers. You have given me wisdom and power, for now you have let me know what we asked of you." The text implies that the prayer was done in the presence of Daniel's friends (2:17, 23b). Did this prayer reveal the public or the private Daniel? Prayer has always been a habit for Daniel. In Dan 6:11, it says, "When Daniel learned that it had been put in writing, he went to his house, in whose upper chamber he had windows made facing Jerusalem, and three times a day he knelt down, prayed, and made confession to his God, as he had always done."

Since Daniel's daily prayers had been a well-known practice in the eyes of the public, it portrayed his public dimension. However, if prayer represents one's limitation and dependence on God, then it also serves as a window to the inner life of Daniel during his public service in the court. I would like to suggest the possibility that prayer fuses both the public and the private Daniel.

Coping Strategies for Immigrants and Minorities in the Profession

As a pastor's wife, ministering to several immigrant churches for the past thirteen years in North America and as an ethnic minority in the profession, I am keenly aware of the journey of disorientation, adaptation, perseverance, and the search for meaning.

I share Leung Lai's sentiment on seeing the book of Daniel as a survival manual. Taking the idea of a survival manual a little further, I think the book of Daniel is specifically pertinent for first-generation immigrants who moved from another country to a new land as their permanent residence. As for the children of these immigrants, who are born and raised in a new land, their situation and challenges may be different from those of the first-generation immigrants. For example, they may want to hide their ethnic origin in order to blend in to the new culture. They may also acculturate more successfully than their first-generation parents. Perhaps they could consider the book of Esther as their survival manual and use the book of Daniel as a reference manual to understand the lived experience of their immigrant parents.

For Further Reading

Hertig, Young Lee, and Chloe Sun, eds. *Mirrored Reflections: Reframing Biblical Characters*. Eugene, OR: Wipf & Stock, 2010.

Kuan, Jeffrey Kah-Jin. "Diasporic Reading of a Diasporic Text: Identity Politics and Race Relations and the Book of Esther." Pages 161–73 in *Interpreting Beyond Borders*. Edited by Fernando F. Segovia. Bible and Postcolonialism 3. Sheffield: Sheffield Academic Press, 2000.

Lee, Jung Young. *Marginality: The Key to Multicultural Theology*. Minneapolis: Fortress, 1995.

Liew, Tat-siong Benny, ed. *The Bible in Asian America*. Semeia 90–91. Atlanta: Society of Biblical Literature, 2002.

Foskett, Mary F., and Jeffrey Kah-Jin Kuan, eds. *Ways of Being, Ways of Reading: Asian American Biblical Interpretation*. St Louis: Chalice, 2006.

CHAPTER 7

Reading Ephesians 6:10–18 in the Light of African Pentecostal Spirituality[1]

J. Ayodeji Adewuya

It has been suggested that "in order to validate its claim to universal validity, the biblical text is dependent on the appropriation of readers with different orientations in different contexts."[2] This suggestion is right. It is akin to what Justin Ukpong describes as "inculturation biblical hermeneutic," an approach by which interpreters consciously and explicitly seek to interpret the biblical text from sociocultural perspectives of different people.[3] This essay is an attempt to do just that.

Without much hesitation, one could say that Eph 6:10–18 is perhaps the clearest and most detailed description in the New Testament of the nature of the spiritual warfare that believers face. It does not assume, but pointedly asserts, that the people of God are engaged in a spiritual warfare. Yet its interpretation, particularly the identity of the enemy and the nature of the warfare, is less than clear due to cultural influences. This essay is one among many others in that trajectory. It demonstrates how the reading of Eph 6:10–18 from an African Pentecostal

---

[1] An earlier version of this essay appeared in *BBR* 22, no. 2 (2012): 251–58.

[2] Bernard C. Lategan, "Scholar and Ordinary Reader: More Than a Simple Interface," in *Reading with African Overtures* (ed. Gerald O. West and Musa W. Dube; *Semeia* 73; Atlanta: Society of Biblical Literature, 1997), 254, as he writes on the interface between the scholar and the ordinary reader in the process of interpretation.

[3] This is a term that is coined by Justin S. Ukpong, "The Parable of the Shrewd Manager (Luke 16:1–13): An Essay in Inculturation Biblical Hermeneutic" in *Reading with African Overtures* (ed. Gerald O. West and Musa W. Dube; *Semeia* 73; Atlanta: Society of Biblical Literature, 1997), 190.

sociocultural and spiritual context[4] not only enhances the understanding of the text but also complements its scholarly interpretation. It consists of a brief review of some of the hermeneutical approaches to understanding the nature of spiritual warfare in Eph 6:10–18 as well as proffers an alternative reading approach that derives from the author's particular African and Pentecostal background. In highlighting my particular background, I seek to show the distinction between Pentecostalism in the northern and southern hemispheres, particularly Africa. In other words, an attempt is made to show a few significant differences between African and North American spiritualities.

An African Pentecostal Spirituality

Because of the transnational character of Pentecostal spirituality[5] and the heterogeneity of Africa, questions can be raised about the propriety of speaking about *African* Pentecostal spirituality. As such, it must be noted that African Pentecostal spirituality is anything but monolithic. Yet there remains a family resemblance among the various strands. One must also recognize its indebtedness and connection to North American Pentecostalism. But while this spirituality is seemingly peripheral in the West in general and in North American life in particular, it offers the dominant conceptual framework in Africa. As Kwabena Asamoah-Gyadu rightly observes, for African Christians in general, categories of power, dominion, and alleviation of suffering by the power of the Holy Spirit are of utmost importance and relevance in the general struggle with fears and insecurities within a universe in which supernatural powers are considered hyperactive.[6]

---

[4] As noted by Daniel Darko in his response in chapter 8, much of what is presented here as an African view of the spirit world has parallels to the Greco-Roman milieu of the New Testament world.

[5] See Rijk A. van Dijk, "From Camp to Encompassment: Discourses of Transsubjectivity in the Ghanaian Pentecostal," *JRAI* 27, no. 2 (1997): 142. He writes, "Pentecostalism is historically a transnational phenomenon, which in its modern forms is reproduced in its local diversity through a highly accelerated circulation of goods, ideas and people. The new charismatic type of Pentecostalism creates a moral and physical geography whose domain is one of transnational cultural inter-penetration and flow."

[6] J. Kwabena Asamoah-Gyadu, "Pulling Down Strongholds: Evangelism, Principalities, and Powers and the African Pentecostal Imagination," *IRM* 96, no. 382/383 (2007): 307. Ephesians 6:10–18 is especially relevant in Africa,

An important and major difference between North American or Western Pentecostalism and that of Africa is in the areas of the work of the Holy Spirit and deliverance from demons. Although the Holy Spirit may have been marginalized in Western theology,[7] it is evident that the presence and activities of the Holy Spirit in and through the community of believers is at the center of African Pentecostal spirituality.

In Africa, rediscovery of the Spirit came at a point of deep crisis and turmoil in its history. Nigeria is a case in point. Pentecostal spirituality flourished at a time of socioeconomic disintegration and political instability in the late 1970s and early 1980s. It was widely embraced because its spirituality offers the resources for dealing with this despair and undertaking the structural adjustment program necessary for the continual search for greater harmony and prosperity for all.

Western critiques of the Pentecostal phenomenon and deliverance from demons quite often fail to take into account the African view of the spirit world. The belief in the existence of other spiritual beings besides God is widespread. In traditional African belief, spirits are ubiquitous: every area of the earth not only has a spirit of its own but also is capable of being inhabited by a spirit.[8] The African universe "is a spiritual universe, one in which supernatural beings play significant roles in the thought and action of the people."[9] The traditional African lives in an intentional world in which things do not happen by chance. Even when the problems are naturally caused, evil spirits are able to set in quickly and exploit the situation to the disadvantage of the victim. The general belief is that events have causes. Unfortunately, as Keith Ferdinando has rightly

---

given the rapid church growth as well as the "strong perception and appreciation of the dynamic supernatural and/or spiritual dimension of the cosmos." Cf. Ernst R. Westland and Salimo Hachibamba, "A Central African Perspective on Contextualizing the Ephesian Potentates, Principalities, and Powers," *Missiology* 3 (2000): 345–46 (341–63).

[7] Jürgen Moltmann, *The Spirit of Life: A Universal Affirmation* (trans. Margaret Kohl; Minneapolis: Fortress, 1992), 83, draws attention to how the Holy Spirit was seen in Protestant theology only as a subjective principle for the appropriation of the salvation won objectively by Jesus on the cross. Norman Pittenger, *The Holy Spirit* (Philadelphia: Pilgrim, 1974), 11–12, sees the marginalization of the Holy Spirit dating back to early Christianity.

[8] E. Bolaji Idowu, *African Traditional Religion: A Definition* (Maryknoll, NY: Orbis, 1973), 175.

[9] Kwame Gyekye, *An Essay in African Philosophical Thought: The Akan Conceptual Scheme* (rev. ed.; Philadelphia: Temple University Press, 1995), 69.

noted, the approach of Western scholarship to issues related to "spirit beliefs" in Africa is "dominated by anti-supernaturalistic rationalism" in which "spirits have no place except as constructions of the human mind."[10] Experiences of demon possession are explained away as either psychological or psychiatric conditions, thus seeing them in terms of mental pathology.[11] E. A. Asamoa's castigation of Western missionaries for their casual and rather dismissive attitude of the effects of evil spirits among Africans societies is on target. He writes:

> It is no exaggeration to say that the church's attitude towards African be-liefs has generally been one of negation, a denial of the validity of those beliefs. ... Anybody who knows the African Christian intimately will know that no amount of denial on the part of the church will expel belief in supernatural powers from the minds of the African people.[12]

Pentecostal spirituality is very much at home in Africa because its interpretation of and responses to evil are continuous with traditional religious ideas in which evil is believed and understood to owe its pres-ence to spiritual causes. It is a worldview in which there is no dichotomy between belief and experience: they always belong together. As a Pen-tecostal minister I can say that the ministries of exorcism, healing, and deliverance have been important tools of evangelization wherever Pen-tecostalism has emerged and thrived. In such contexts, believers see the existential meaning of Christ's ministry in their lives.[13] Clinton Arnold's description of the rhetorical setting of Ephesians in Asia Minor is, with-out doubt, largely applicable to many similar situations in present-day Africa. He writes, "Many converts were streaming into the churches—converts who were formerly affiliated with the Artemis cult, practiced magic, consulted astrologers, and participated in various mysteries Un-derlying the former beliefs and manner of life of all these converts was a common fear of the demonic powers."[14]

---

[10] Keith Ferdinando, *The Triumph of Christ in African Perspective: A Study of Demonology and Redemption in the African Context* (PBTM; Carlisle: Pater-noster, 1999), 70.

[11] Cf. Paul Radin, *Primitive Religion: Its Nature and Origin* (New York: Vi-king, 1937), 131–32, as noted by Ferdinando, *The Triumph of Christ*, 71.

[12] E. A. Asamoa, "The Christian Church and African Heritage," *IRM* 175, no. 45 (July 1955): 297.

[13] Asamoah-Gyadu, "Pulling Down Strongholds," 308.

[14] Clinton E. Arnold, *Ephesians, Power, and Magic: The Concept of Power in Ephesians in Light of Its Historical Setting* (Grand Rapids: Baker, 1992), 122.

Hermeneutical Approaches to Ephesians 6:10–18

Rudolf Bultmann's quest for the demythologization of the New Testament is well known and, as such, does not need to be rehashed here. However, its continued relevance for the understanding of the evil powers in Eph 6:10–18 is of importance. For Bultmann, supernatural powers, unlike what obtains in the African worldview, do not have the ability to interrupt the natural realms of cause and effect. Thus he comes to the conclusion that the biblical language on the spirit world is nothing but a mere objectification of the transcendent into the immanent. The Holy Spirit is not an expression for a personal Being, but rather a way of describing "authentic Christian living." To Bultmann, living "according to the Spirit" does not refer to any supernatural influence. Rather, it describes "a genuine human life" that lives out "of what is invisible and non-disposable and, therefore, surrenders all self-contrived security."[15] For someone to accept a contrary view is not to have "grasped the hiddenness and transcendence of divine action and . . . seek God's action the sphere of what is worldly."[16]

Bultmann does not appear to be alone, and his view is somewhat reflective of people in the western hemisphere who downplay the existence of real evil forces that wreak havoc in the world. For example, Markus Barth argues that the evil forces refer to "the world of axioms and principles of politics and religion, of economics and society, of morals and biology, of history and culture."[17] In his recent work, Timothy Gombis follows this line of reasoning.[18] Having dismissed the point of the passage as either addressing the issue of the victorious Christian life or what he describes as "frighteningly speculative engagements with demonic forces," he writes that "the enemy of the church is not the world or the people in the world but the powers" and that "our warfare involves resisting the corrupting influences of the powers" in a subversive manner.[19]

---

[15] Rudolf Bultmann, *Jesus Christ and Mythology* (trans. Schubert M. Ogden; New York: Scribner's, 1958), 17.

[16] Rudolf Bultmann, *New Testament and Mythology and Other Basic Writings* (trans. Schubert M. Ogden; Philadelphia: Fortress, 1984), 122.

[17] Markus Barth, *The Broken Wall: A Study of the Epistle to the Ephesians* (Vancouver: Regent College Publishing, 1959), 91.

[18] Timothy G. Gombis, *The Drama of Ephesians: Participating in the Triumph of God* (Downers Grove, IL: InterVarsity Press, 2010), 159.

[19] Ibid.

Other scholars have taken the opposite view of the demythologization of evil powers that is espoused by Bultmann. Instead, they argue for
the reality of spiritual forces in some form or the other. For example, on
the one hand, Wesley Carr argues that the spiritual powers in Eph 6:12
are not demonic, evil, or malicious. Instead, Carr argues, the powers
refer to angelic powers.[20]

Carr's view has been rightly challenged both for lack of evidence
and for methodological inconsistencies.[21] By contrast, Walter Wink
maintains that the evil powers in Eph 6:12 refer to "the inner and
outer aspects of any given manifestation of power . . . the *spirituality* of
institutions."[22] Wink also denies the existence of a personal being called
the devil, insisting that it is a "collective symbolization of evil" and "the
collective of weight of human fallenness."[23] Whatever Wink cannot
categorize materially, he labels as superstitious.[24] As Annang Asumang
rightly observes and succinctly states:

> Where Wink erred was to deny any particular influence of personal spirits
> in implementing the stratagems of the evil powers. In so doing, not only
> is the teaching in Ephesians undermined, the negative effects of increased
> spiritism, witchcraft, and occultism in some societies are ignored. Conse-
> quently, Wink more-or-less creates a new myth of the existence of imper-
> sonal spirits whose effects are corporate and not personal. He commits a
> not infrequent mistake of the Cartesian enlightenment philosophy that
> regards any other worldview as "primitive and unscientific."[25]

---

[20] Wesley Carr, *Angels and Principalities: The Background, Meaning, and
Development of the Pauline Phrase* αἱ ἄρχαι καὶ αἱ ἐξουσίαι (SNTSMS 42; Cambridge: Cambridge University Press, 1981).

[21] See, among others, Clinton E. Arnold, "The 'Exorcism' of Ephesians 6:12 in
Recent Research: A Critique of Wesley Carr's View on the Role of the Evil Powers
in the First Century AD Belief," *JSNT* 30 (1987): 71–87; Walter Wink, *Naming the
Powers: The Language of Power in the New Testament* (Philadelphia: Fortress, 1984);
P. T. O'Brien, "Principalities and Powers: Opponents of the Church," in *Biblical In-
terpretation and the Church: Text and Context* (ed. D. A. Carson; Exeter: Paternoster,
1984), 110–50, esp. 125–28; and R. A. Wild, "The Warrior and the Prisoner: Some
Reflections on Ephesians 6.10–20," *CBQ* 46, no. 2 (1984): 284–85.

[22] Wink, *Naming the Powers*, 5.

[23] Walter Wink, *Unmasking the Powers: The Invisible Forces That Determine
Human Existence* (Philadelphia: Fortress, 1986), 43.

[24] Kabiro wa Gatumu, *The Pauline Concept of Supernatural Powers: A Reading from an African Worldview* (PBM; Eugene, OR: Wipf & Stock, 2009), 184.

[25] Annang Asumang, "Powers of Darkness: An Evaluation of Three Hermeneutical Approaches to the Evil Powers in Ephesians," *Conspectus* 5 (March 2008): 13.

In contrast to the preceding views, Arnold is correct in asserting that "Paul never showed any sign of doubt regarding the real existence of the principalities and powers. He saw them as angelic beings belonging to Satan's kingdom. Their aim is to lead humanity away from God through direct influence on individuals as well as through wielding control over the world religions and various other structures of our existence."[26] He also cautions us against the tendency to forget Paul's sociocultural context. Paul was a man of his times. Paul believed in the personal character of the powers of evil in the universe. The idea here is much the same as in 2 Cor 10:3–4: "For though we walk in the flesh, we do not war according to the flesh." It is irrelevant if the particular opponent we face is a principality, a power, or a ruler of the darkness of this age. Collectively, they are all members of spiritual hosts of wickedness in the heavenly places. They are all part of a spiritual army that is organized and established into ranks—and under the headship of Satan, the devil, who comes against us with his wiles.

In Eph 6:12 Paul brings together again three of the four words for power previously used in 1:19 and 3:16–21. The Ephesians would have understood the implications. The same power that raised Jesus from the dead (1:20) and brought them to life when they were dead in trespasses and sins (2:1) is now available to them. There can be no doubt about its adequacy. Believers are to clothe themselves with the armor that only God provides. It is a complete outfit because the soldier must be fully protected. Paul does not call the believer to enter into spiritual warfare. He simply announces it as a fact. The fact that our real battle is not against flesh and blood is lost on many Christians, who put all their efforts in that direction.

Ephesians 6:10–18 in African Pentecostal Hermeneutics

Healing and exorcism take place in the context of what Pentecostals describe as spiritual warfare.[27] This is based on Paul's submission, "For

---

[26] Clinton E. Arnold, *Powers of Darkness: Principalities and Powers in Paul's Letters* (Downers Grove, IL: InterVarsity Press, 1992), 169.

[27] In most cases the reading or hearing of Eph 6:10–20 focuses on exorcism, as this essay does. However, this writer recognizes the fact that the world of the Ephesians to whom the letter was addressed as well as that of Africans was one that was obsessed with mystical and spiritual power that sought to understand, control, and benefit from or defend against it in one's daily life and the welfare of the community. In other words, the meaning of Eph 6:10–20 must

our struggle is not against flesh and blood but against the rulers, the authorities, against the powers of this dark world and against the spiritual forces of evil in the heavenly realms" (Eph 6:12). As noted by Kwesi Dickson and Paul Ellingworth, "for the African, the world of spirits is a real world. . . . It is the spiritual beings which actually control the world; indeed the world is a spiritual arena in which the various categories of spiritual beings display their powers. Man [*sic*, humanity], in particular, is entirely dependent upon these spiritual beings."[28] Thus, it is understood that a person who manifests a certain behavior is under the control of or has been taken possession by an invisible being or power.

Among the Yoruba of southwest Nigeria, Satan is known as *Esu*. He is known to be the trickster deity and is regarded as a divinity of mischief who can make things difficult for humankind and divinities. He is malicious and a mischief maker, quite capable of causing confusion, bringing about complicated situations, or promoting malice among people. As Bolaji Idowu observes, "There is an unmistakable element of evil in Esu and for that reason he has been predominantly associated with things evil."[29] It is quite clear still that the Yoruba put almost every evil tendency and practice among human beings down to his agency.[30] Idowu continues, "From all accounts he is not only a bewilderingly versatile character but also extremely capricious. He is an elusive, slippery character whom it is not easy to fix."[31] The preponderance of evil associated with Esu leads Idowu to equate him with either the devil or Satan. When a person behaves in a wicked way, he or she may be referred to as "omo esu," that is, a child of the devil or being used of the devil. The Yoruba avoid having any dealings with Esu. Instead they offer sacrifices to avoid or elude his wickedness, callousness, and devilish atrocious plans, believing that victory is possible. This view ultimately informs African Pentecostal spirituality that situates the possibility of victory in the sacrifice of Christ. One always hears such songs as:

---

be understood as broader than exorcism. It demands, as Daniel Darko suggests, that the reader must understand ethics as imperative in spiritual warfare.

[28] Kwesi A. Dickson and Paul Ellingworth, "God, Spirits, and the Spirit World," in *Biblical Revelation and African Beliefs* (ed. Kwesi A. Dickson; London: Lutterworth, 1969), 36.

[29] E. Bolaji Idowu, *Olodumare: God in Yoruba Belief* (London: Longman Group, 1962), 83.

[30] Ibid.

[31] Ibid., 85.

I have seen, seen the downfall of Satan
Glory be to God, glory be to Jesus
I have seen, seen, seen the downfall of Satan,
Glory be to God. Amen.

I have seen, seen, the victory of Jesus,
Glory be to God, glory be to Jesus,
I have seen, seen, the victory of Jesus
Glory be to God. Amen.

To use Matthew Ojo's language, Pentecostals have "appropriated their traditional cultural backgrounds,"[32] and in doing so they have defined salvation in a holistic sense that includes healing and deliverance from demonic attacks and oppressions. As such, Eph 6:11–20 may have unwittingly become an integral part of the African Pentecostal's tenet of faith.

Apart from Satan, the Yoruba have strong belief in mysterious powers, which are called various names, such as *oogun, egbogi,* or *isegun* (magic, medicine); *oso, oogun ika,* or *oogun buburu* (sorcery, bad magic); and *aje, eye, or oso* (witchcraft). Sorcery is the use of bad or evil magic to kill or harm people or to cause misfortune to people or the society. This use can be out of spite or to avenge a wrong done. Some types of sorcery include *abilu* (evil magic that brings a drastic change in the fortune of a person), *apeta* (invocation shooting), *efun* (evil magic that makes a person behave abnormally), and *isasi* (evil magic that makes a person act as one who is insane).

Witchcraft is the utilization of certain inherent psychic powers in people to cause harm or havoc to people or property. It is a willpower, emanating from within people, for the purpose of achieving evil ends without the use of any tangible apparatus. Both sorcery and witchcraft are regarded as a reality among the Yoruba. They are usually regarded as forces of evil and used as explanations of social tensions and misfortunes in the society. If one is found to be a witch or wizard within the society, the spirit must be exorcised from the person in order to avoid endangering the life of the individual or the community. One should not therefore wonder why passages like Eph 6:10–18 and 2 Cor 10:4 are some of the passages often quoted by African Pentecostals. When

---

[32] Matthew A. Ojo, *The End-Time Army: Charismatic Movements in Modern Nigeria* (Asmara, Eritrea: Africa World Press, 2006), 202.

Paul speaks about wrestling with "principalities and powers" or having an "agent of Satan" in his body, he speaks in categories and idioms that are at home with African cosmological ideas. It is not surprising that Pentecostal preachers in Africa, keenly aware of the African worldview about spirits, have seized on that worldview to espouse the doctrine and practice of deliverance from demons.

Conclusion

In concluding this essay, one must take note of C. S. Lewis's warning in his introduction to *The Screwtape Letters*. He writes, "There are two equal and opposite errors into which our race can fall about the devils. One is to disbelieve in their existence. The other is to believe, and to feel an excessive and unhealthy interest in them. They themselves are equally pleased by both errors, and hail a materialist and a magician with the same delight."[33]

It is evident that the biblical worldview of spiritual causality within which African Pentecostal spirituality finds its roots resonates strongly with African worldviews on cause and effect as it relates to evil in the world, including demon possession and the spirit world. As I have argued, even problems that may be considered natural can be taken advantage of by evil spirits for the purpose of exploiting such to their advantage. So when Paul speaks about wrestling with "principalities and powers," he speaks in a language that immediately resonates with an African, and even more so with an African Pentecostal. Nevertheless, one must be wary of the tendency by many Africans to unduly elevate evil powers and attribute everything to demons. In such cases the result is nothing less than a systemization of evil powers in the world, something that is beyond what Paul intended to do. Moreover, a situation whereby human beings are reduced to pawns in the battle between good and evil spirits and for which their responsibility is only limited to prayer and deliverance is not biblical.

For Further Reading

Asamoa, E. A. "The Christian Church and African Heritage." *IRM* 44, no. 175 (1955): 292–301.

---

[33] C. S. Lewis, *The Screwtape Letters* (Oxford: Macmillan, 1962), 3.

Asamoah-Gyadu, J. Kwabena. "Pulling Down Strongholds: Evangelism, Principalities and Powers and the African Pentecostal Imagination." *IRM* 96, no. 382–383 (2007): 306–17.

Ferdinando, Keith. *The Triumph of Christ in African Perspective: A Study of Demonology and Redemption in the African Context*. PBTM. Carlisle, England: Paternoster, 1999.

Gatumu, Kabiro wa. *The Pauline Concept of Supernatural Powers: A Reading from the African Worldview*. PBM. Milton Keynes, England: Paternoster, 2008.

Ojo, Matthew A. *The End-Time Army: Charismatic Movements in Modern Nigeria*. Asmara, Eritrea: Africa World Press, 2006.

CHAPTER 8

Response: Moral Standing as a Community or Individual Exorcism in Ephesians 6:10–20?

Daniel K. Darko

Professor Adewuya provides an ideological reading of Eph 6:10–20, emerging from the history of interpretation of "principalities and powers," in the perspective of an African Pentecostal. He provides an overview of his framework and observes three major developments in the study of the powers in the New Testament: the view that demythologizes the powers along the lines of Bultmann (also Markus Barth and Timothy Gombis); a reading of the powers as angelic forces or sociopolitical powers, notably by Wesley Carr and Walter Wink; and the school that defines and interprets the powers as personal spiritual forces. It is in this third understanding that he establishes a suitable framework for an African reading. I have made a few observations from his presentation that may be worthy of consideration, and I present them here in no particular order.

Parallels in African and Greco-Roman Cosmology

It is apparent that much of what is presented as an African view of the spirit world has close parallels with a Greco-Roman world concept. Jews, Greeks, and Romans shared a worldview in which spiritual beings were active in the sphere of humans and in human affairs. Moreover, devotion to the gods and dependence on spiritual powers for protection and prosperity were commonplace in the social context of Ephesians in Asia Minor. Even the elite engaged in astrology, magic, and ancestral worship.[1] What is deemed African spirituality, for the most part, is akin

---

[1] According to Cicero, "the aim of *cultus* was to gain the favor of the gods (*pax deorum*) and avert their anger." He recounts the overwhelming influence

to the worldview of the early Christians. In Ephesians, wholeness is a spiritual blessing and salvation includes deliverance from the control of "the ruler of the powers of the air" (2:1–3).

The Boundaries of Demon Hunting and the Biblical Framework

The essay aptly sketches African spirit cosmology and engages African scholars based in Africa in a commendable fashion. For the sake of the Western reader or hearer, the extremes associated with this worldview among African Christians could have been addressed in the main discussion. The hunt for demons everywhere and the fear of evil omens from bizarre sources would have benefited from ample treatment to clarify the scope and boundaries. It is no secret that "no one dies of a natural cause in West Africa, even among Christians"—death and adversity are almost always linked to a spiritual cause.[2] Professor Adewuya briefly observes this at the end of his essay. However, ample treatment of the subject matter and recommendations for curbing exploitation and spiritual abuse would have eased some concerns of skeptics and shown reasonable boundaries of expression of Christianity in this framework.

---

of augurs and astrologers in the Roman culture (*On Divination* 1:12–25). Ancestral worship or rituals to dead ancestors were common in Greco-Roman antiquity. "Ovid describes two festivals in honor of the dead, the Parentalia and Feralia, that were celebrated from 18–21 February. He reports the reputed origins of these practices, while also recounting several rituals that involve sympathetic magic." See Valerie Warrior, *Roman Religion: A Sourcebook* (Focus Classical Sources; Newburyport, MA: Focus & R. Pullins, 2002), 31, and Ovid *Fasti* 2.533–570.

[2] See E. Kingsley Larbi, *Pentecostalism: The Eddies of Ghanaian Christianity* (Accra: SAPC, 2001); J. Kwabena Asamoah-Gyadu, *African Charismatics: Current Developments within Independent Indigenous Pentecostalism in Ghana* (SRA 27; Leiden: Brill, 2005); and Kwame Bediako, *Jesus and the Gospel in Africa* (Maryknoll, NY: Orbis, 1970). These scholars (also from West Africa) have shown that what I call "spirit cosmology" in Africa informs how Christianity is received and practiced across denominational lines in the region. Asamoah-Gyadu is a Methodist minister; Bediako was a Presbyterian minister; Larbi is a Pentecostal minister. All three scholars have demonstrated that the Christian Bible would have no meaning or relevance to the West African unless it takes into account the worldview being explained by Adewuya and interprets the text to meet the prevailing fear of demonic powers and the need to be protected from diabolic forces.

Defining the Nature of the Warfare, Not Just the Opponent

The observer may note that the African Pentecostal eye (Adewuya) saw "exorcism" as soon as it found "spiritual warfare" in the text. Conversely, the passage locates the theater of spiritual warfare in concrete ethics, and this is particularly significant in the ongoing discussion.

First, it may serve to caution the African tendency to overspiritualize events and recognize that ethics (truth, righteousness, faith) is where the spiritual battle to maintain a standing with God occurs in Ephesians. Second, the emphasis on individual exorcism departs from the communal framework of the pericope. The passage rather suggests the necessity for *the community*, not *an individual* demoniac, to combat spiritual threats. Third, an African parallel could be drawn from how curses are invoked in African traditional religion as punitive retaliation against ethical violations that seem to yield real spiritual consequences. Thus, the African reader may observe ethics as imperative in spiritual warfare, without negating exorcism as a means of deliverance for some converts to Christianity. Exorcism is however not the focus of this passage.

Implications for Biblical Scholarship

There are a few implications to these observations for Western evangelical scholars as well as non-Western scholars based in the West.

First, I suggest that we bring the biblical worldview of the spirit world to the forefront of our conversation in hermeneutics since trends in global Christianity suggest a link between this worldview and church growth. The emphasis on prayer, spiritual warfare, and healing in non-Western Christianity is rooted in this world concept. Western scholarship is losing credibility in this regard as our scholarship is increasingly perceived as "peer talk" with no substantial contribution to faith in the transcendent. Even our foreign students who return home are sometimes branded "evangelicals without power" and portrayed as a threat to church growth due to "misguided" notions of scholarship and "Bultmannian" readings of biblical texts.[3]

---

[3] I have observed a common discomfort in some Western institutions when Africans, Asians, or Latin Americans propose to do their doctoral thesis about this subject matter. In some cases, research students had to move to other institutions to complete their projects or produce a thesis that contradicts their

Second, non-Western scholars based in the West may need to gather courage to discuss openly our worldview and show how they shape our interpretative lenses.[4] Such conversation may include the abuse and ignorance that we find in superstitions on one hand and extreme Western charismatic influence on the other.

Third, biblical scholars are far behind the growing trend in witchcraft, Wicca, and *Santería* among the general public in the West. More so, the immigrant churches are importing this worldview to the West, hence the need for discussion on the biblical view of spiritual beings in the light of non-Western cultures. I suggest that evangelical scholars lead the way in this endeavor as part of our service to the church.

For Further Reading

Asamoah-Gyadu, J. Kwabena. *African Charismatics: Current Developments within Independent Indigenous Pentecostalism in Ghana.* SRA 27. Leiden: Brill, 2005.

Bediako, Kwame. *Christianity in Africa: The Renewal of Non-Western Religion.* Maryknoll, NY: Orbis, 1997.

Gatumu, Kabiro wa. *The Pauline Concept of Supernatural Powers: A Reading from the African Worldview.* PBM. Milton Keynes, England: Paternoster, 2008.

Sugirtharajah, R. S. *Postcolonial Reconfigurations: An Alternative Way of Reading the Bible and Doing Theology.* St. Louis: Chalice, 2003.

————, ed. *Voices from the Margin: Interpreting the Bible in the Third World.* 3d ed. Maryknoll, NY: Orbis, 2006.

---

honest position on the subject matter to satisfy their supervisors or directors. I tell my African students, "they call it real scholarship" in our Western universities and seminaries. We may want to revisit this notion of scholarship that stands alongside a decline in church growth, explore different worldviews that others bring into the discussion, and participate in scholarship that is open to other viewpoints and critical analysis thereof.

[4] Craig S. Keener. *Miracles: The Credibility of the New Testament Accounts* (2 vols.; Grand Rapids: Baker Academic, 2011). Keener's compilation of miracle stories and his compelling examination of the history of interpretation of the miracles and the weaknesses thereof may serve as an invitation for a serious dialogue on how worldviews and Christian experiences inform or should inform our reading of the text.

CHAPTER 9

The Bible as Specimen, Talisman, and Dragoman in Africa: A Look at Some African Uses of the Psalms and 1 Corinthians 12–14[1]

Grant LeMarquand

In 2006 Edwin Yamauchi delivered the presidential address, entitled "Scripture as Talisman, Specimen, and Dragoman," at the fifty-eighth meeting of the Evangelical Theological Society (ETS). The paper was published in *JETS* the next year.[2] In his essay, Professor Yamauchi described "three contrasting attitudes"[3] taken toward the Bible. As we shall see, I think that there may in reality be more than three attitudes toward Scripture on offer, but this typology seems a helpful heuristic device for beginning an analysis of various African uses of Scripture. Yamauchi makes only a passing reference to Africa in his essay, interestingly in his relatively brief discussion of Scripture as a talisman. Our discussion will begin with the least common way in which Scripture is read and used in Africa.

Specimen

The predominant mode of studying the Bible in the European and North American biblical guild is the "Scripture as a specimen" mode. For approximately the last two hundred years, historical analysis of the biblical text has dominated scholarly discussion. The Enlightenment roots of historical-critical scholarship have been and continue to be discussed,

---

[1] An earlier version of this essay appeared in *BBR* 22, no. 2 (2012): 189–99.
[2] Edwin M. Yamauchi, "Scripture as Talisman, Specimen, and Dragoman," *JETS* 50, no. 1 (2007): 3–30.
[3] Ibid., 3.

and I will not rehearse the modern history of exegesis here.[4] A few brief points will suffice.

First, it should be said that for all the good and helpful effects of the historical-critical method (close analysis of the historical contexts that gave rise to the text, careful attention to the text itself) there can be little doubt that, for better *and* for worse, historical scholarship emphasizes the gap between our world and the biblical world. The professional biblical scholar is trained and socialized to read the Bible "like any other book," even if the evangelical scholar may believe in her heart that it is *not* like any other book.

Given my unease concerning the guild's one-sidedly historical emphasis, it was with some hope that I read Bruce Chilton's preface to the first issue of the *Bulletin for Biblical Research*:

> The Institute for Biblical Research has launched the *Bulletin for Biblical Research* as an instrument for understanding the religious senses of scripture . . . [it will be] . . . fully critical. . . . Yet current practice does not often acknowledge that religious meaning was the obvious context in which scriptural documents were produced, and the medium within which they were transmitted and received.[5]

My initial reaction to Chilton's statement was to cheer. Since my earliest days as an undergraduate in a religious studies program, I have been concerned that both theology and (ironically) religion seemed to have been sidelined by the biblical studies guild. The *BBR* announcement gave me hope. Sadly, I must confess, although the *BBR* has produced many fine and valuable studies over the years, I cannot say that it has lived up to the promise on page 1 of its first journal. Most of what I read there are studies of a more or less modernist historical-critical type, which reach more conservative conclusions about the text than more liberal journals might.

Historical-critical scholarship is also a reality in Africa. Most African scholars are trained in Western exegetical methods. Most African biblical scholars do their doctoral work in Europe or North America. Even the few who study in the fledgling graduate programs in Africa are reading Western texts most of the time. A major difference, however, is that there

---

[4] As a typical example see Werner Georg Kümmel, *The New Testament: The History of the Investigation of Its Problems* (trans. S. M. Gilmour and H. C. Kee; Nashville: Abingdon, 1972 [1970]).

[5] Bruce Chilton, Preface, *BBR* 1 (1991), 1.

are very few doctoral dissertations written by Africans that make no explicit reference to some African context. In the 1980s John Mbiti could identify only two works, which he misleadingly described as "pure" biblical scholarship, by which he meant works that do not explicitly cite an African issue as the motivation for study or make reference to an African situation within the text of the study itself.[6] There are now many more works by African scholars which *appear* on the surface to be scholarship for scholarship's sake—but time after time, when I have discussed their work with African scholars, I have found that their dissertation director or their publisher had steered them away from drawing religious or theological conclusions for the sake of the church and the people of Africa.

One example will suffice. There have been several studies written by Africans on Paul's discussion of spiritual gifts in 1 Cor 12–14. Discussions of the spiritual gifts and their use and abuse in the African context can be found in the commentaries by Samuel Abogunrin, Dachollom Datiri, and Ayodeji Adewuya.[7] Articles on this subject have been authored by Justin Ukpong, Chris Ukachukwu Manus, and Chris Obi.[8] A doctoral dissertation by Luke Ndubuisi on *Paul's Concept of Charisma in 1 Corinthians 12* discusses the use of spiritual gifts in the African Roman Catholic context in some depth.[9] Another dissertation, however,

---

[6] John S. Mbiti, *Bible and Theology in African Christianity* (Nairobi: Oxford University Press, 1986), 49. On Mbiti's comment see Grant LeMarquand, "New Testament Exegesis in (Modern) Africa," in *The Bible in Africa: Transactions, Trajectories, and Trends* (ed. Gerald O. West and Musa W. Dube; Leiden: Brill, 1980), 84–86.

[7] Samuel Oyinloye Abogunrin, *The First Letter of Paul to the Corinthians* (African Bible Commentaries; Nairobi: Uzima, 1988); Dachollom Datiri, "1 Corinthians," in *Africa Bible Commentary* (ed. Tokunboh Adeyemo; Grand Rapids: Zondervan, 2006), 1377–98; J. Ayodeji Adewuya, *A Commentary on 1 and 2 Corinthians* (London: SPCK, 2009).

[8] Justin S. Ukpong, "Charisms and Church Authority: A New Testament Perspective," in *Authority and Charism in the Nigerian Church: Proceedings of the 8th National Theological Conference Held at the National Missionary Seminary of St. Paul Gwagwalada—Abuja (FCT)* (ed. Kris Owan; Abuja: Catholic Theological Association of Nigeria, 1993), 39–44; Chris Ukachukwu Manus, "Authority and Charism: New Testament Notes and Pastoral Implications in the Nigerian Church," in ibid., 45–60; Chris A. Obi, "Charismata and Authority: A Pauline View," in ibid., 110–24.

[9] Luke Nbubuisi, *Paul's Concept of Charisma in 1 Corinthians 12: With Emphasis on Nigerian Charismatic Movement* (EUS 765; Frankfurt: Peter Lang, 2002).

Prophecy and Tongues: A Pauline Theology of Charismata for Service in the Church [1 Cor. 14] by Donatus Udoette, makes no reference to Africa or to any contemporary context.[10] The thesis is simply a reconstruction of Paul's message for the first-century Corinthian situation. It is exegetical and historical. When I asked the author if that was his only goal, his response was that he had written a final chapter that attempted to bridge the gap between the Pauline message and his contemporary Nigerian set- ting, but his supervisor required him to remove it. In the same year that his thesis was published, he published a journal article that contained the substance of that final excised chapter.[11]

The study of Scripture as a specimen, which turns the Bible into a mere archaeological artifact, is not a popular endeavor in Africa. It is perhaps significant that the only two African scholars known to me who make no explicit attempt to use their biblical research for the good of their continent both teach in North America. The study of the Bible as merely a specimen to help in the reconstruction of history is known but rarely done by African biblical scholars.

Talisman

Yamauchi's lecture at ETS in 2006 mentioned Africa in the follow- ing way: "Magic is still quite prevalent in many places of the world today such as the Caribbean and Africa."[12] True enough. Yamauchi goes on to point out that the world of the Bible was itself pervaded by magic and magical ideas, describing archaeological evidence of ancient prophylac- tic amulets and incantations involving biblical texts and suggesting that some of the characters in Scripture may have held magical ideas.

---

[10] Donatus Udoette, *Prophecy and Tongues: A Pauline Theology of Charis- mata for Service in the Church [1 Cor. 14]* (Rome: Collegio San Pietro, 1993).

[11] Donatus Udoette, "Towards a Theology of Charismata for the Nigerian Church," *Encounter: A Journal of African Life and Religion* 2 (1993): 16–28. This is not an isolated example: J. Ayodeji Adewuya's published dissertation (*Holi- ness and Community in 2 Cor. 6:14–7:1: Paul's View of Communal Holiness in the Corinthian Correspondence* [Studies in Biblical Literature 40; Leiden: Brill, 2003]) makes several mysterious references to Africa, which seem to point to the presence of an African hermeneutical section in the book, but such a sec- tion of the book is not to be found. When asked, the author confessed that the publisher had insisted on removing that section of the work.

[12] Yamauchi, "Scripture as Talisman, Specimen, and Dragoman," 3.

But we do not need to return to the biblical, classical, or medieval periods to find uses of Scripture, which might be described as "magical." The term "talisman" is an appropriate way to describe how many people in Africa think of the Bible. Indeed, considering the Bible as in some sense a sacred object is not uncommon even in the secular West.

In Africa, the use of the Bible as a sacred object is more pervasive. The biographer of John Chol Daau, a young South Sudanese man who spent his childhood as a refugee, describes John's earliest encounter with the Bible this way. As a baby John had trouble sleeping through the night and would cry for hours on end. A relative, who was one of the first Christians in the area, was visiting. Hearing of the boy's problem, he held his Jieng language[13] New Testament over John's eyes and said, "Hey, boy, instead of crying you will proclaim this book . . . look at the book." John reached for the New Testament and grabbed it. His crying stopped, and they left the Bible in the crib with him, declaring that his name should be "John" after John the Baptist. The biographer continues, "What they had witnessed was not simply a little baby gripping a story with a message, but rather John as an infant had inherited an object of power."[14]

Justin Ukpong, a Nigerian Roman Catholic scholar, has written a helpful report on field research from Port Harcourt, Nigeria, on "popular" use of the Bible in that area. The word "power" is a key term in Ukpong's report. It seems that the Bible is understood by many ordinary Christians in Africa as an object that contains intrinsic power: a fetish or a talisman. Even those who cannot read may place a Bible in their purse or under their pillow for good fortune.

Of course, the Bible is widely understood in Africa as containing a message about God's love and grace, which brings salvation and spiritual support. The Bible is also considered a weapon to be used in spiritual warfare for combating evil forces such as demons.[15] The African worldview is not compartmentalized in the same way that it is in the West. The

---

[13] In the West, the Jieng people are most often called Dinka.

[14] Lilly Sanders Ubbens, "Chasing after the Cross: The Early Life of Rev. John Chol Daau" (MAR thesis, Trinity School for Ministry, Ambridge, PA, 2011), 5.

[15] For scholarly investigation of this subject, see Keith Ferdinando, *The Triumph of Christ in African Perspective: A Study of Demonology and Redemption in the African Context* (PBTM; Carlisle: Paternoster, 1999); Michael Olusina Fape, *Powers in Encounter with Power. Paul's Concept of Spiritual Warfare in Ephesians 6:10–12: An African Christian Perspective* (Glasgow: Mentor, 2003); Anthony Iffen Umoren, *Paul and Power Christology: Exegesis and Theology of Romans*

Bible is used, according to Ukpong, in prayer for long life, prosperity, good health, and success in exams. Ukpong explains:

> No distinction was ... made between the use of the bible for spiritual needs and for material needs. Prosperity, happiness, good health, etc. are regarded as a sign of divine blessing, while a life of depravation on earth is a negation of the expected happiness of the afterlife. There is therefore no purely spiritualized interpretation of the Bible.[16]

But what does it mean to use the Bible in prayer for all of these things? African use of the Psalms provides an instructive focus. A number of important studies have been produced in recent years on the popular use of the Psalms in African Christianity. African Instituted Churches[17] have, as a common factor within their great diversity, openness to African cultural practices, which may be considered suspect in the mission-founded churches. In some of these churches the psalm texts, together with incantations (often the reciting of divine names) and sacred objects, are employed within a prescribed rite for the purpose of achieving a desired goal. In his booklet *The Mystic Power of the Psalms*, E. O. Nwokoro, of the Aladura Church, prescribes various psalms to be read with particular procedures. For example, in order to have success in business, the one praying should read Psalm 8: "At sunset ... into pure olive oil for 3 days and rub on your face and hands after ... prayer."[18] "To avert danger on your journey and to gain 'Great Men's/Women's' favour. Read [Psalm 21] before leaving home for the journey or interview, facing the East in your private room [using] the Holy Name—Jehovah Jehhakki."[19]

1:3–4 in Relation to Popular Power Christology in an African Context (NTSCC 4; Frankfurt: Peter Lang, 2008).

[16] Justin S. Ukpong, "Popular Readings of the Bible in Africa and Implications for Academic Readings," in *The Bible in Africa: Transactions, Trajectories, and Trends* (ed. Gerald O. West and Musa W. Dube; Leiden: Brill, 1980), 590.

[17] African Instituted Churches are African denominations that have either broken away from mission-founded churches or have sprung up, apparently independently of any foreign missionary activity. The bibliographical data on such groups is immense. The title (and subtitle) of an older work on the subject is instructive: David B. Barrett, *Schism and Renewal in Africa: An Analysis of Six Thousand Contemporary Religious Movements* (Nairobi: Oxford University Press, 1968).

[18] E. O. Nwokoro, *The Mystic Power of the Psalms: On Selected Chapters for Daily Use* (Calabar: ESUBOM, 1994), 6.

[19] Ibid., 7.

Some formulas are much more complex. For the casting off of evil spirits, for example, Nwokoro prescribes the following: "Fill a new earthen bowl with running water, put 7 palm fronds, recite [Psalm 29] 10 times [with] the Holy Name Ahha-Jehovah over the water and bathe the person possessed and he/she will surely be freed. If this is observed for 3 days with fasting, the person who caused the effect on the possessed will openly confess and regret his/her action."[20] The use of water, candles, oil, and recitation in particular places at particular times, the repetition of the ritual, fasting, washing, and other actions are used in conjunction with praying the designated psalms. Nwokoro makes no mention of why particular things are used or, indeed, why particular psalms are to be used. His booklet simply provides formulas to be used with no allusion to the psalm's meaning. The booklet promises that answers to prayer will be given for those seeking relief from headaches, fever, or fractures, to punish a witch or wizard, to help with concentration or understanding, to cure snake or scorpion bites, as well as bullet and bite wounds, to avert mishaps, to quit smoking, to release a detainee, to draw nearer to God, and many other requests.[21]

Other groups, however, are interested in how *the message* of some psalms can be effective. Especially interesting is the wide use of the imprecatory psalms. Although Western scholars and Christians are, to say the least, vexed by psalms that call down curses on enemies and

---

[20] Ibid., 8.

[21] Daniel K. Darko pointed out the similarity between these practices of some African Instituted Churches and formulas in eighteenth- and nineteenth-century European magical texts, especially those found in *The Sixth and Seventh Books of Moses*, a collection of magical rites and incantations published in various forms in Germany and northern Europe and widely disseminated in African-American communities in the southern United States and the Caribbean—and in Anglophone West Africa, where they were popular in Masonic circles. Although these European texts do not use the Psalms, the use of mysterious "divine names" and formulas for various rites bears a distinct similarity to some of the formulas used by Nigerian African Instituted Churches. Elizabeth Isichei reports that in the "1920s there were regular advertisements in the Nigerian press for *The Sixth and Seventh Books of Moses* and for other occult literature" and that although "it has been denounced by Aladura leaders as magical and pagan ... there is, within some prophetic churches, an enduring attraction towards 'gnosis'" (*A History of Christianity in Africa: From Antiquity to the Present* [Grand Rapids: Eerdmans, 1995], 295).

ask God to take vengeance on evildoers, some African Christians find
these passages helpful.

David Adamo sees this use of the Psalms in the African context "as
a legitimate response to victimization."[22] Adamo points out that traditional African culture understands misfortune of all kinds to have social
and spiritual causes. For example, although the Western understanding
of malaria—that one contracts this disease from being bitten by an in-
fected mosquito—is generally accepted, this scientific explanation may
not answer all of the African person's questions. The deeper questions
will be: "Why did *I* get sick, but my sister sitting in the same room did
not?" "Who wished me ill and so sent the mosquito?" Given this worldview, the cure for malaria provided by the dispensary may not be enough.
An enemy may have sent the disease, and so a trip to the local traditional
healer may also be needed to discern the ultimate first cause, whether
that cause be a living person, an ancestor, or a demonic force.

Even African Christians have not always found Western answers
sufficient and so have often reverted to traditional African solutions.
African Instituted Churches have attempted to baptize these traditions,
as it were, and use the Scriptures as means of protection from and over-
powering of enemies of all sorts. And so an African Christian may carry
a Bible for protection, or write verses from the Psalms on the side of
his vehicle, or put psalm verses into amulets. The imprecatory psalms
are not seen as embarrassing artifacts from a more vengeful Israelite
past but as a resource to combat the real evils that one faces every day.
For example, the Prophet J. O. Ogunfuye recommends that Ps 7 (Ps
7:1 reads, "O Lord, my God, in you do I take refuge; save me from my
pursuers and deliver me") be written out on a piece of paper and placed
in a consecrated bag and kept under one's pillow, together with a prayer
of protection.[23] Adamo argues that these practices reveal a real trust in
the power of God's Word, which is sharper than any two-edged sword:

---

[22] David Tuesday Adamo, "The Imprecatory Psalms in African Context," in
Biblical Interpretation in African Perspective (ed. David Tuesday Adamo; Lanham,
MD: University Press of America, 2006), 141. Adamo's *Reading and Interpreting
the Bible in African Indigenous Churches* (Eugene, OR: Wipf & Stock, 2001) does
a good job of laying out the data of the mechanics of how African Instituted
Churches use the Psalms therapeutically, and for protection and success. Adamo's book, however, provides little to help us analyze or interpret these practices. The 2006 article is much more helpful in carrying the discussion forward.

[23] Adamo, "The Imprecatory Psalms in African Context," 147.

"Unlike the Western world," he says, "where the Bible is in doubt and the Bible ceases to be the Word of God."[24]

In answer to the possible objection that such use of the imprecatory psalms may encourage vengeful thinking, which could lead to vengeful action, Adamo asserts that

> African Christians use imprecatory Psalms . . . as an expression of God's righteous anger against injustice. . . . They believe that they are taking the offender or the enemies to the court of God. . . . Admittedly, care must be taken in the use of the imprecatory Psalms for evil intention. It should only be used for God's vengeance. . . . All things must be submitted to God with humility and understanding that God is a righteous God.[25]

It should be noted that this is not the only way in which African Christians understand or use the Psalms and that there is a growing bibliography of psalm studies in African biblical scholarship.[26]

---

[24] Ibid., 150.

[25] Ibid., 151. Cf. the cautionary notes in Solomon Olusola Ademiluka, "The Use of Imprecatory Psalms in African Context," *AJBS* 23, no. 2 (2006): 53–62; Jace R. Broadhurst, "Should Curses Continue? An Argument for Imprecatory Psalms in Biblical Theology," *AJET* 23, no. 1 (2004): 61–90; David G. Firth, *Surrendering Retribution in the Psalms: Responses to Violence in the Individual Complaints* (PBTM; Milton Keynes: Paternoster, 2005); and Marta Høyland Lavik, "Killing Children with God's Permission? The Rhetoric of Retaliation in Psalm 137," in *Culture, Religion, and the Reintegration of Female Child Soldiers in Northern Uganda* (ed. Bård Mæland; BTA 10; New York: Peter Lang, 2010), 193–206.

[26] Recent African scholarship on the Psalms includes Ernst R. Wendland, *Comparative Discourse Analysis and the Translation of Psalm 22 in Chichewa, a Bantu Language of South-Central Africa* (SBEC 32; Lewiston, NY: Edwin Mellen, 1993); Anastasia Boniface-Malle, "Interpreting the Lament Psalms from the Tanzanian Context: Problems and Prospects" (PhD diss., Luther Seminary, 2000); Felix Chingota, "Interpretation of the Psalms: A Concentric Approach," *MJBS* 1 (2003): 9–18; H. Efthimiadis-Keith, "Is There a Place for Women in the Theology of the Psalms? Part I: An Investigation into the Female Imagery of the Ancient Hebrew Psalter," *OTE* 12, no. 1 (1999): 33–56; idem, "Is There a Place for Women in the Theology of the Psalms? Part II: Self-expression and the 'I' in the Ancient Hebrew Psalter," *OTE* 17, no. 2 (2004): 190–207; Stephen Egwim, "Decolonizing the Lament Psalms: A Reading of Psalm 109 in African Context," in *Decolonization of Biblical Interpretation in Africa* (ed. S. O. Abogunrin et al.; BSS 4; Ibadan: Nigerian Association of Biblical Studies, 2005), 192–219; Emmanuel Francis Yankum Grantson, "Death in the Individual Psalms of Lament: An Exegetical Study with Implications for Theology and Mission" (ThD diss.,

It may strike the Western reader that these uses of the Psalms verge on or cross over the border into magic. That may be so—if so, there are certainly dangers that must be avoided! It may be true, however, that some characters in the biblical story seem to participate in magical thinking: the bleeding woman who secretly sneaks up behind Jesus to steal her healing by touching his clothing may be one (Mark 5:25–34; Matt 9:20–22; Luke 8:43–48)—and yet she is healed and Jesus calls her attitude "faith," even if we may want to say that her faith is somehow incomplete or imperfect.[27]

It may also be that those who apply the imprecatory psalms in this fashion have paid insufficient attention to Jesus' teaching about vengeance and nonretaliation: that enemies are to be loved, not cursed (Matt 5:38–48).

I am left wondering, however, whether Western Christians (even orthodox evangelical Christians) do not sometimes stray into *trivializing*

Lutheran School of Theology, 1991); B. Kafang Zamani, "A Semantic and Theological Investigation of the Concept of 'Poor' in the Psalms" (PhD diss., Trinity International University, 1993); Liswanisu Kamuwanga, "Exile and Suffering: Reading Psalm 77 in African Context," *OTE* 20, no. 3 (2007): 720–35; idem, "Prayer for Protection: A Comparative Perspective on the Psalms in Relation to Lozi Traditional Prayers," *OTE* 21, no. 3 (2008): 670–91; Hannah Kinoti, "Psalm 23:1–6: An African Perspective," in *Return to Babel: Global Perspectives on the Bible* (ed. John R. Levison and Priscilla Pope-Levison; Louisville: Westminster John Knox, 1999), 63–68; Z. Kotzé, "The Witch in Psalm 59: An Afro-centric Interpretation." *OTE* 21, no. 2 (2008): 383–90; Besem Oben Etchi, "Psalm 31 at the Service of Women Dragged into Sex Work in Cameroon," *Hekima Review* 44 (2011): 55–65; Ignatius M. C. Obinwa, *Yahweh My Refuge: A Critical Analysis of Psalm 71* (EH 839; Frankfurt: Peter Lang, 2006); C. O. Ogunkunle, "The Suffering of the Messiah: A Reflection on Psalm 22 in the African Context," in *Christology in African Context* (ed. S. O. Abogunrin et al.; BSS 2; Ibadan: Nigerian Association of Biblical Studies, 2003), 41–53; Pauline Otieno, "Interpreting the Book of Psalms in the Coptic Orthodox Church in Kenya," in *Interpreting the Old Testament in Africa: Papers from the International Symposium on Africa and the Old Testament in Nairobi, October 1999* (ed. Mary N. Getui, Knut Holter, and Victor Zinkuratire; BTA 2; New York: Peter Lang, 2001), 159–64; Wenceslaus Mkeni Urassa, *Psalm 8 and Its Christological Reinterpretations in the New Testament Context: An Inter-Contextual Study in Biblical Hermeneutics* (EUS 23/577; Frankfurt: Peter Lang, 1998).

[27] For a discussion of this text, see Grant LeMarquand, *An Issue of Relevance: A Comparative Study of the Story of the Bleeding Woman (Mk 5:25–34; Mt 9:20–22; Lk 8:43–48) in North Atlantic and African Contexts* (BTA 5; New York: Peter Lang, 2004).

our relationship to the sacred text. An African student of mine has a Bible in which he will not underline and which he treats very carefully. He tells me that when he is talking with Muslim friends, he is careful to use that Bible, because Muslims are frequently shocked at how Christians treat their Bibles. Placing coffee mugs on top of a sacred text or defacing it by underlining and marking it up strikes Muslims as treating a holy book with insufficient respect.

I suspect that another category besides "talisman" is needed in this discussion. Is it possible, for example, to consider the Bible to be a sacred item without falling into viewing it magically? Can we consider the Bible as a kind of sacrament, an item, a physical object, through which heaven touches earth? Perhaps the use of the Bible in more liturgical churches portrays this attitude to the Bible—some churches include the Bible or parts of the Bible (a Gospel book, for example) in processions, holding the text high in the air as it is brought down from the holy table into the midst of the people to be read. Other churches (which perhaps do not think of themselves as highly liturgical) display an open Bible on the Lord's table or some other prominent place. We need not fall into magical thinking to see the Bible as a thing set apart for holy use, and therefore as an object deserving of respect and care.

If we say that we approach God's Word with awe and wonder, perhaps we should approach the outward form of God's Word in ways that reflect our inward respect. Within Judaism, of course, the Torah is treated with awe and even joy. For example, "On Simchat Torah, congregations traditionally take each Torah scroll out of the Holy Ark, awarding their worshipers with the honor of embracing the Torah while dancing around the bima, or podium, from which the weekly portion is read."[28] In Eastern Orthodox churches the Bible is often kissed by worshipers.

A few years ago, in an ecumenical institution in Canada, a professor delivering a lecture in an introduction to the New Testament class wanted to impress upon his students the *mere* humanity of the Bible. Standing on a copy of the Bible at the front of the class, he noted that no lightning had descended from heaven. To his surprise, however, his disrespectful action *did* cause a reaction within the student body, and the leaders of the constituent colleges of the institution were forced to rethink their association in various ways: perhaps some of the attitude

---

[28] http://www.israelnationalnews.com/News/News.aspx/139827 (accessed March 7, 2011).

to the book as a sacred object still lingers even in the West. And that is not necessarily a bad thing.

Dragoman

Yamauchi's final category is "dragoman," an archaic term (from the Arabic *terjuman,* an interpreter or translator) that Yamauchi uses to refer to the Scripture as interpreter and to the reader as seeking guidance through careful study. The Scripture as a text that interprets us and which is interpreted for the sake of life, is the main approach to the Bible which can be found in Africa. A few African interpreters can be found who seem only to be interested in the Bible as a specimen, and there are many examples of a more magical, talisman-like use of the Bible. The majority of readers, however, approach the text for guidance, for life in the midst of the often dangerous and chaotic world of Africa.

And so, for example, 1 Cor 12–14 is seen as a passage that can guide the church to encourage the use of gifts of the Holy Spirit as well as to regulate the use of those gifts. Ndubuisi, for example, agrees with the charismatic movement within the Nigerian Roman Catholic Church that 1 Cor 12–14 encourages the use of tongues, prophecy, and other gifts such as healing, but he cautions that there are also dangers. There are "manipulative tendencies" that come with charismatic authority that is independent of established church hierarchy;[29] the so-called gifts of ecstatic utterance can be used in a confusing way, but Paul is careful to teach that God is a God of peace (1 Cor 14:33) and that everything should be done decently and in order (1 Cor 14:40);[30] and that, in the end, the purpose of the gifts is to build up the body of Christ in love ("Paul's main concern in 1 Cor 12–14 is the unity and the upbuilding of the body and it is not by accident that this great hymn of love, chapter 13, stand between chapters 12 and 14").[31]

Similarly, Abogunrin understands 1 Cor 12–14 as both an encouragement to use the gifts of the Spirit and a cautionary warning to those who would misuse them. Concerning the gifts of healing (1 Cor 12:9), he writes, "A gospel which emphasizes the salvation of souls alone is unbiblical and meaningless within the African context. God is not only

---

[29] Ndubuisi, *Paul's Concept of Charisma,* 221.
[30] Ibid., 234.
[31] Ibid., 249.

the Saviour of souls but also of bodies. The power to heal through prayer and the laying on of hands is a gift for every age."[32]

At the same time he cautions, "Paul says that there is need for orderliness and this is a major problem with many of the African Indigenous Churches, mission Pentecostal churches and various Church youth organizations."[33] In other words, African Christian readers are for the most part uninterested in viewing the Bible as a mere specimen of historical interest. Most of those who write about the Bible shy away from a magical, talisman approach to Scripture. They approach the Bible as a source (usually "the source") of spiritual guidance.

The same could be said of those who write on the book of Psalms. Although ordinary Christians may sometimes employ the Psalms magically, most see the Psalms as God's provision of comfort, wisdom, and guidance. Writing in the *Africa Bible Commentary*, Anglican bishop Cyril Okorocha says,

> Psalms are read in many mainstream Protestant churches across Africa each Sunday as one of the three readings from Scripture. Besides this use in corporate worship, they are also often used in individual worship, in small group fellowships, in Bible studies, and in family devotions at home. They have a special place in our hearts because they are easy to study, to preach and teach from, and to store in our hearts. They are enjoyable to recite and sing as hymns, songs, and choruses. They are practical and down to earth. While most of the Bible speaks to us about God and God's ways, the Psalms help us to speak to God. They are not given to us to be used as magic formulae. Rather they draw us near to God and help us to cry out to him in our times of need and to praise him as he deserves. Praise the Lord![34]

Obviously, Okorocha is aware of the temptation in the African context to use the Psalms magically, but his words point toward using the Psalms devotionally and theologically rather than magically. The Psalms can function as a dragoman—interpreting God to the believer, and the believer to God.

Teresa Okure, a New Testament scholar who is also a Roman Catholic sister, quotes an Ibibio proverb that says that "the legs of the bird that

---

[32] Abogunrin, *The First Letter of Paul to the Corinthians*, 131.

[33] Ibid., 127.

[34] Cyril Okorocha, "Psalms," in *Africa Bible Commentary* (ed. Tokunboh Adeyemo; Grand Rapids: Zondervan, 2006), 607.

flies in the air always point to the ground (*Inuen afruroke ke enyong ukot asiwot isong*)."[35] She appeals to the professional biblical guild[36] to pursue scholarship in the service of *life.*

> Biblical criticism took off from the ground and remained poised in flight for a greater part of the twentieth century. In the process it all but lost touch with life on the ground as it explored various imaginative ways of reconstructing the biblical texts and their contexts. Scholarship now needs to land on the ground, reconnect with life and critically assess its aerial view findings for the benefit of life on the ground.[37]

Biblical criticism that does not labor for the good of the church and of the world is truly a dead letter. For this reason African biblical scholars are explicit that they are reading the Bible with their commitments and interests declared up front. They do not hide their hopes that their scholarship may have some kind of small impact on a suffering world. They do not write merely for the sake of scoring debating with their fellow scholars. Africa's problems are many, and they are serious: HIV/AIDS, famine, desertification, political instability, war, ethnic tension, gender inequality. The Bible is not silent about these issues. Biblical scholars who claim to follow the God of life should not ignore the groanings of creation all around us as we study, teach, and write.

For Further Reading

Adamo, David Tuesday. "The Imprecatory Psalms in African Context." Pages 139–54 in *Biblical Interpretation in African Perspective*. Edited by David Tuesday Adamo. Lanham, MD: University of America Press, 2006.

LeMarquand, Grant. "African Readings of Paul." Pages 488–504 in *The Blackwell Companion to Paul*. Edited by Stephen Westerholm. Hoboken, NJ: Wiley, 2011.

———. "Siblings or Antagonists? The Ethos of Biblical Scholarship from the North Atlantic and African Worlds." Pages 61–85 in *Bib-

---

[35] Teresa Okure, "'I will open my mouth in parables' (Matt 13.35): A Case for a Gospel-Based Biblical Hermeneutics," *NTS* 46, no. 3 (2000): 463.

[36] Okure's essay was the main paper delivered at the Society for New Testament Studies meeting in Pretoria in 1999 (ibid., 445).

[37] Ibid., 463.

lical Interpretation in African Perspective. Edited by David Tuesday
   Adamo. Lanham, MD: University Press of America, 2006.
Ndubuisi, Luke. *Paul's Concept of Charisma in 1 Corinthians 12: With
   Emphasis on Nigerian Charismatic Movement.* European University
   Studies 23/765. Frankfurt am Main: Peter Lang, 2002.
West, Gerald O., and Musa W. Dube, eds. *The Bible in Africa: Transac-
   tions, Trajectories and Trends.* Leiden: Brill, 2000.

CHAPTER 10

Response: Promises and Questions of Reading the Bible in Africa

Osvaldo Padilla

I would like to thank Dr. LeMarquand for his stimulating essay. It reached me at a time when I had been reading and reflecting on both the importance of our situatedness in the interpretation of Scripture and the contribution of non-Western readings of Scripture.[1] Dr. LeMarquand's piece has provoked further reflection.

There are a number of thoughts in this essay with which I resonated deeply. Given limitations of space, I can concentrate on only one. In particular, I suggest that it is difficult to read his piece and *not* come away with the realization that we have a profound need of scholars from regions outside the Western world engaging the biblical text. There are many reasons for this, but I shall concentrate on the one below.

In many cases the social, economic, and religious ethos of numerous countries outside the Western world share significant overlap with the world of the Bible (in my case in particular, I think of the world of the New Testament). Therefore, scholars from these regions may have a certain facility inhabiting at least some areas of the biblical text, which scholars from other regions may not possess. This thought stems from the assumption that biblical interpretation is never done from an abstract position, a point well explained in Dr. LeMarquand's section on the Bible as specimen. If this is the case, the contributions of African and other scholars from the non-Western world are essential, not least in the aid that they can provide in buttressing our trust in the Scriptures. Recall

---

[1] For the latter I have found the works of Philip Jenkins, *The Next Christendom: The Coming of Global Christianity* (rev. ed.; Oxford: Oxford University Press, 2007) and Lamin Sanneh, *Whose Religion Is Christianity? The Gospel Beyond the West* (Grand Rapids: Eerdmans, 2003) most helpful.

that one of the reasons why the credibility of the Bible has been questioned in the Western world is its sheer otherness—not only in matters of culture and the miraculous but also in its morality. I therefore find Dr. LeMarquand's example of the way in which the imprecatory psalms are being read by some African Christians very helpful. These Christians, by virtue of the region in which they live, have been shamed, violated, and even killed by their enemies. The imprecatory psalms are real for them. To quote Dr. LeMarquand, these psalms are seen "not as embarrassing artifacts from a more vengeful Israelite past, but as a resource to combat the real evils that one faces every day." And, quoting this time from David Adamo: "African Christians use the Imprecatory Psalms . . . as an expression of God's righteous anger against injustice. . . . They believe that they are taking the offender or the enemies to the court of God,"[2] as they repeat these imprecatory psalms in their prayers. For many Christians in the West, although this interpretation of the imprecatory psalms may be reached, it is done so perhaps only at the theoretical level. The African reading, by contrast, emerging as it does from powerlessness and spilled blood, provides a new dimension of conviction about the interpretation of these psalms. Read from the African context, these psalms make sense in a way that may not be the case in other contexts. Can Western scholars afford to ignore these vital contributions?

And yet, in many of our evangelical scholarly and publishing circles, I rarely see a biblical commentary (to mention one medium of biblical scholarship) written by Africans or Hispanics or Asians. I find it very disappointing that there are commentary series with the word "international" in their titles when almost all the authors are British, North American, or Australian. Can we call this "international" in the age we are living in? Do not misunderstand. I would be just as disappointed if all the authors were Africans or Hispanics. The point is that biblical interpretation can suffer from a kind of provincialism when non-Western voices are not brought to the table.[3]

---

[2] David Tuesday Adamo, "The Imprecatory Psalms in African Context," in *Biblical Interpretation in African Perspective* (ed. David Tuesday Adamo; Lanham, MD: University Press of America, 2006), 151.

[3] I am reminded of the following observation concerning one of the main reasons for F. C. Baur's radical interpretation of early Christianity, namely, provincialism: "Baur lived in a small German university town. Of all that was going on in Germany he had an acute awareness; to the rest of the world he seems to have paid less attention" (Stephen Neil and Tom Wright, *The Interpretation*

There are, however, a few questions that should be raised about some of the proposals of this essay. First, in the section on the Bible as talisman, it was not clear to me where Dr. LeMarquand drew the line between the Bible as sacred object and the Bible as amulet. For example, he mentions the African practice of reading the Psalms along with incantations and the reciting of divine names in order to obtain a desired prayer request. This seems to me to be a potential contradiction of Matt 6:7: "When you are praying, do not heap up empty phrases as the Gentiles do; for they think that they will be heard because of their many words." As Jesus is instructing his disciples how to pray, he provides a negative example that is found in the practice of the Gentiles.[4] They "heap up empty phrases,"[5] thinking that in this way they will be able to manipulate the deity and thus secure their petition. By contrast (6:8), the disciples have a loving heavenly Father who already knows their needs even before they pray. There is thus no need to engage in verbal manipulation. To engage in this type of activity, therefore, is an insult both to the sovereignty of God and to his goodness. I wish Dr. LeMarquand had been more direct in his assessment of the legitimacy of this practice in some African churches.

Second, although I agree with Dr. LeMarquand that not enough academic works are written that at the same time address theological issues for the sake of the church in Africa, I was left with the impression that he may—perhaps inadvertently—be driving a wedge between scholarship and contextualized theology. What does he mean, for example, when he says that "there are now many works by African scholars which appear to be scholarship for scholarship's sake"? What does "scholarship for scholarship's sake" mean? Does this mean that exegesis that does not *immediately* address the local ecclesial context is misguided? Should evangelicals, therefore, not engage in, say, textual criticism because there may not be an apparent immediate payoff for the local church? There is a potential danger in coming to the text of Scripture to find answers for

---

of the New Testament, 1861–1986 [2d. ed.; Oxford: Oxford University Press, 1988], 22).

[4]This practice was also used by Jews. See now Gideon Bohak, *Ancient Jewish Magic: A History* (Cambridge: Cambridge University Press, 2008), 70–143.

[5]This phrase translates the Greek verb βατταλογέω, a term that does not appear with frequency in Greek literature. When it does, it is usually dependent on the New Testament. BDAG, s.v., has the gloss: "use the same word again and again."

our immediate, local problems without at the same time recognizing that the text may not *directly* address the contemporary problem. When this is not recognized, we may be led to believe that the hermeneutical walls separating us from the text of Scripture can be instantly evaporated; but the result may be a domestication of the biblical text. Without the painstaking research that sometimes does not provide immediate answers, we end up with (for example) a Jesus who looks just like us. The Jesus that emerges is the Jesus of modern liberalism, which, ironically, is one that is distasteful to most African Christians.

It is time to sum up. Dr. LeMarquand has called our attention to the wonderful contribution that African believers can provide to the church in the Western world in interpreting Scripture. He gave the example of their understanding of the imprecatory psalms. I suggested that *one* of the reasons why African (and other non-Western) Christians can provide such helpful readings of biblical texts is that they inhabit a world that in many areas (persecution, economics, religious ethos) is not that foreign to the biblical world. The gap may not be as wide. But this advantage, if we are not careful, can ironically turn into a disadvantage. We may disvalue the necessity of rigorous scholarship. This can lead to a domestication of God. In addition, the danger of syncretism (as seen perhaps in the use of incantations in prayer) is particularly pressing. Dr. LeMarquand has presented an informative and stimulating essay. I am eager to see future publications from him in this area that can also address some of the problems I have raised in this response.

For Further Reading

Adeyemo, Tokunboh, ed. *Africa Bible Commentary*. Grand Rapids: Zondervan, 2006.

González, Justo L. *Santa Biblia: The Bible through Hispanic Eyes*. Nashville: Abingdon, 1996.

Oden, Thomas C. *How Africa Shaped the Christian Mind: Rediscovering the African Seedbed of Western Christianity*. Downers Grove, IL: InterVarsity Press, 2008.

Ruiz, Jean-Pierre. *Reading from the Edges: The Bible and People on the Move*. Maryknoll, NY: Orbis, 2011.

Sanneh, Lamin. *Whose Religion Is Christianity? The Gospel Beyond the West*. Grand Rapids: Eerdmans, 2003.

Index of Modern Authors

Index of Scripture and Other Sources